a Williams Lea company

CW00732852

Not Another Digital Transformation

The 10XGeneration

Ady Kalra
Mary-Beth Hosking

Published by TSO (The Stationery Office), part of Williams Lea,
and available from:

Online
www.tsoshop.co.uk

Mail, Telephone & E-mail
TSO
PO Box 29, Norwich, NR3 1GN
Telephone orders/General enquiries: 0333 202 5070
E-mail: customer.services@tso.co.uk
Textphone: 0333 202 5077

© Quantum Transformation, trading as 10×Generation, 2024

All figures, graphics, logos and designs used within this title ("**Work**") have copyright of Quantum Transformation, trading as 10×Generation.

No part of the materials in this Work, including graphics and/or logos, may be copied, photocopied, reproduced, translated or reduced to any electronic medium or machine-readable form, in whole or in part, without specific permission in writing from TSO. Applications to reuse, reproduce and/or republish any material in this Work should be sent in writing to TSO at 18 Central Avenue, St Andrew's Business Park, Norwich NR7 0HR with an email to: commissioning@williamslea.com

Notice of Liability
The contents in this Work and anything contained in it are distributed "As Is", without warranty of any kind, either express or implied, including but not limited to, implied warranties for its quality, performance, merchantability or fitness for any particular purpose. Neither Quantum Transformation, trading as 10×Generation, nor the publisher, its employees, agents, dealers and/or distributors shall be liable to any end user(s) and/or third parties with respect to any liability, loss and/or damage caused and/or alleged to have been caused directly and/or indirectly by the contents of this material or any parts thereof, and the aforementioned parties disclaim all such representations and warranties and assume no responsibility for any errors, inaccuracies, omissions or any other inconsistencies herein.

This Work may include hyperlinks to third-party content, advertising and websites, provided for the sake of convenience and interest. Neither Quantum Transformation, trading as 10×Generation, nor the publisher endorse any advertising and/or products available from external sources and/or any third parties.

Trade marks
Quantum Transformation, trading as 10×Generation, reserves all rights.

ISBNs
Print: 9780117094574
PDF: 9780117094581
ePub: 9780117094598

SD000139

Contents

About the authors

Ady Kalra

With extensive experience in guiding technology teams, Ady Kalra has been on a continual journey of mastering and adapting modern product engineering and innovation practices over his 16-year career. Armed with a master's degree in Computer Applications, he ardently champions the quest for knowledge and perpetual learning.

Throughout his professional trajectory, Ady has consistently remained at the forefront of emerging technology trends and novel approaches to crafting resilient technical organizations. He presently leads global architecture and engineering teams, facilitating seamless interactions with global executive teams and CEOs of business units.

Ady's unwavering conviction lies in forging close collaborations with the business and technology stakeholders, instilling a DevSecOps mindset and ensuring that the engineering team harmonizes seamlessly with the overarching business vision. Notable among his recent accomplishments is a comprehensive transformation project that introduced a groundbreaking operating model, resulting in a 100% self-sustained organizational culture, thus empowering teams and enabling global scalability.

Mary-Beth Hosking

Mary-Beth Hosking began her writing journey in 2019 when she wrote her first book, *In One Piece: A step by step guide to surviving change*, which was published in the middle of the Covid pandemic and was designed to support leaders through significant change. In 2023, she completed her second book, *When Now Means NOW! A handbook for career change, advancement and progression*, focusing on her byline: 'Don't be afraid to pivot, be afraid not to'.

During this time, Mary-Beth had accepted the role of global CIO and met Ady Kalra while working in the same business. Their collaboration for the 10×Generation came about when the two were discussing the pitfalls many organizations face when in a growth phase. With a combined experience of more than 35 years in the technology industry, they knew that there must be a better way to support growth from a startup to an enterprise without overburdening teams with cumbersome processes and bloating the business with unnecessary headcount.

Mary-Beth holds a master's degree in Business and Technology with majors in Strategic Management and Organizational Change Management, and has experience of leading restructures in multinational organizations. She acts as a mentor, coach and leader to those in the midst of organizational uncertainty, and has successfully delivered major programmes during times of significant change.

Foreword

Awareness is the greatest agent for change.

Eckhart Tolle[1]

We confront a monumental shift at the intersection of technology, business and humanity. This era, fuelled by AI, productivity leaps and exponential growth, challenges us to rethink our approach to 'digital transformation'. The phrase, once a buzzword for cloud integration, now symbolizes a comprehensive cultural and strategic revolution.

The publication you hold isn't just another guide on cloud computing or IoT (internet of things) integration. It's a compass to navigate the tumultuous seas of change. Ady and Mary-Beth, through this groundbreaking work, provide a North Star for innovation, guiding companies to not just adapt but thrive in this new landscape. They emphasize that burying one's head in the sand is not an option. The statistics are stark: digitally transformed companies are 26% more profitable and hold a 12% higher market valuation. Ignoring these figures is a risk no leader can afford to take.

Not Another Digital Transformation is a clarion call for leaders at every level. Whether you're at the helm of a startup or steering a large enterprise, the challenge is universal: how to keep up with the relentless pace of change. This guide offers a holistic strategy, touching upon the necessity of shifting mindsets and skillsets, understanding the voice of the client, and fostering a culture that doesn't just withstand change but leverages it for growth and innovation.

Change is daunting, but stagnation is far worse. This publication is your guide to creating sustainable change and future-proofing your organization. It's an invitation to become a 10×Generation visionary leader, to embrace the blistering pace of change, and to harness the potential of artificial superintelligence, robotics and automation. The question is, will you rise to this challenge, or will you be left behind in the sands of complacency? The choice is yours.

Alan Smithson

Founder, METAVRSE

Preface

In the summer of 2022, Ady Kalra and Mary-Beth Hosking began working together: Ady as the head of engineering and Mary-Beth as the CIO for a global gaming organization. During the first six months of working together, it became apparent that both leaders had a similar goal: to take the organization from a startup to an enterprise model without overburdening it with superfluous process and additional headcount.

At the time, the business was reeling from the pressures of the 'great resignation', and the war on talent had impacted the velocity of the development teams. Costs to secure high-end technical talent were becoming prohibitive, and the regulatory requirements in the industry were creating unforeseen bottlenecks.

While working on various programmes in the business, Ady and Mary-Beth knew that there was a better way to address productivity in the IT teams and, more importantly, across the entire business ecosystem. This radical approach would ultimately flip the idea of DevSecOps (development, security and operations working cohesively), Agile (as per the Agile method of accelerated development), the Spotify model (working in small, discrete teams to increase development timelines) and all other current methodologies on their head, and possibly polarize the organization.

With their complementary strengths, they realized that they would be able to bring together best practices to increase the velocity of their teams in support of the business, and explore the overhaul of current business thinking. This would create a virtuous feedback loop across the business, with IT solidly at the forefront of the change, not just as an enabler.

The barrier that they faced, however, was aligning the business with this new way of working. Even though the operational layer* was re-aligned, the other layers in the business were not, and this lack of clarity about what the other layers were doing was having an impact. It was then that Ady and Mary-Beth decided to write their first book on how to prepare an organization for rapid action, giving rise to the idea of the 10×Generation.

The 10×Generation is a method by which an entire organization is brought together with the same level of autonomy, visibility and alignment. All teams and individuals are aware of the strategic direction of the organization, and how they need to contribute towards achieving the desired overall outcomes. The term '10×Generation' is derived from the authors' need to show organizations that it is possible to achieve exponential growth (growing not from 1 to 2 but from 1 to 10, then from 10 to 100, and so on).

The 10×Generation is an unapologetic response to the wastage[2] experienced across all organizations as they attempt to relive the heydays of their startup roots. From the time a startup receives funding, the process of bloat begins, with the founders thinking

---

* The term 'operational layer' is interchangeable with 'operational view', as is 'tactical layer' with 'tactical view' and 'strategic layer' with 'strategic view'.

potentially of exit strategies and the newly appointed executives feeling the pressure to produce and grow the business to satisfy venture capitalists. This leads to an increase in headcount and the creation (under the guise of governance) of over-burdensome processes as the steady pace to underperformance begins.

For some, who may have experience only of the enterprise organization, the reality may display an already distended workplace where barriers to success are the norm. Here communication is stifled by red tape and delivery is hampered by politics, resulting in a lack of cohesion across the business. What should be a virtuous cycle of growth, visibility and prosperity has become bogged down with excess, empire building, command and control, and layers of bureaucracy. A world so far from the 10×Generation of massive action and throughput, that if the organization survives its first five years, its velocity has decreased significantly and it is rapidly moving towards the first of many digital transformations. This becomes a precarious situation for those leaders who are looking for substantial growth in their chosen market.

This publication, therefore, is targeted at all leaders, whether they are technical leaders, line managers or members of the C-suite. It is positioned to provide a game plan, regardless of the size and maturity of an organization. The plan focuses on increased productivity, improved visibility, and alignment of strategy to ensure that everyone in the business knows exactly how to improve overall velocity and reduce glut.

This is not only a guide for technology organizations, but for all organizations influenced and supported by technology. When thinking about an organization's growth aspirations, there is a need to rethink the path currently taken by re-imagining it as a way to achieve the 10×Generation state. This is a place of exponential quantity, quality and growth. It represents the aspirational state or the 'North Star', and is where your organization wants and needs to be.

The following section uses an analogy to exemplify the journey.

The 10×Generation journey

Think of the last plane flight you went on. There were three key milestones that took place for you to get in the air (see Figure 1).

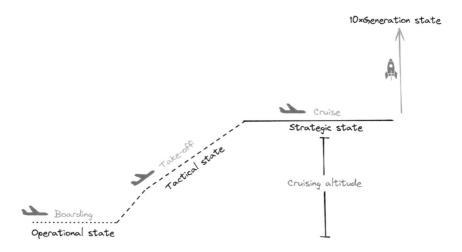

Figure 1 The 10×Generation journey

Stage 1: Boarding

Before boarding, you know exactly where you are going, because your tickets show you. You have checked in for the flight and have boarded the plane with the other passengers. On the ground, there are baggage handlers loading the plane with luggage, there are ground crew ensuring the safety of everyone on board, and on the flight deck are pilots checking the route to the destination.

In the control tower, there are flight controllers monitoring the airport and other flights, ensuring that when the time comes it is safe to take off. You sit down, fasten your seat belts and wait for the safety demonstration, and no matter how many times you've flown before, you still half-listen, just in case.

At every step of the way you have a clear understanding of your place on the plane. You know where the exits are, you know where you are going, and you know you are surrounded by other people who are on the same journey as you.

In the 10×Generation, we consider this stage the *operational state*. This is where you are preparing for take-off. This is where the ground crew of your organization resides: the engine room or technology hub. This is generally seen as the technical epicentre, with those people who ideate, create and support your technology aspirations. That team that is always there in the background, making sure everything runs smoothly.

Stage 2: Take-off

The plane gently pulls out from the gate, the safety demonstration is over and the flight crew is preparing the cabin for take-off. This is the next milestone in getting you airborne and on your way. The ground crew is still in the background, supporting the flight, ensuring a clear runway and clear skies ahead, but you don't think about that.

You look out of the window and watch ground slip past as you wait for the inevitable torque as the plane accelerates, faster and faster, 120 mph, 150 mph, flaps set down to reduce drag; eventually it hits the sweet spot, 180 mph, and the plane lifts.

The curve is steep and gets steeper as the plane pushes into the air, taking you higher and higher as you push to reach cruising altitude. You watch and wait for the elusive seat belt sign to be turned off, but you know you must reach cruising altitude before the pilots will allow this to happen.

In the 10×Generation, we consider this next stage the *tactical state*. This is where the in-flight crew takes over – the onboard crew whose members are readying themselves to help you on your journey. This represents the support functions in the organization, including people and culture (P&C), finance, learning and development, marketing, and administration – all the functions that provide an enjoyable flight. On a long-haul flight, this is where your comfort will take precedence: the crew will ensure that all meals are served and cleared away as efficiently as possible to enable you to sleep. In the world of business, this is where processes need to be streamlined, where visibility across the functions will reduce bottlenecks and will create a virtuous support cycle. This will provide both the operational and strategic teams with functional assistance.

Stage 3: Cruising altitude

Finally, the ding is heard, signifying that you have reached cruising altitude. Then the cabin manager announces: 'Ladies and gentlemen, the captain has turned off the "Fasten seat belts" sign.'

You have made it. Cruising altitude. You are now on your way. This is the time when you can watch the flight path, understand where the pilots are taking you, and sit back and watch the in-flight entertainment. Refreshments are served and you can relax; you can freely move about the cabin and enjoy the flight.

This is where you want to be. Soaring through the sky at 500 mph. You will reach your destination in no time at this rate.

In the 10×Generation, this is the *strategic* state. This is where everyone knows where they are travelling and how fast they are going in order to get there. Everyone on the plane, all travelling together – knowing that the ground crew are still there in the background ensuring safety and support, knowing that the in-flight crew will make the flight comfortable.

When all three stages are aligned, the flight will proceed on its path and land at its destination on time every time.

Stage 4: Going exponential

To ensure that your flight is on track, you will need to create a culture of growth and support. This can be done only by ensuring that everyone, across all three layers, has visibility of each other, and that they are all aligned.

Too many times, a change is thrust upon an organization that focuses only on one layer. When this happens, you have the 'wheel of chaos': another digital transformation that may appear on the surface to be delivering the desired change but, beneath the surface, is failing as individuals return to old ways of working.

To get to this next stage, you need to rethink the passenger airliner analogy. You don't just want to continue taking long-haul flights to the same destinations, do you? Change is needed, with both a top-down and bottom-up approach. Everyone needs to be invested in the new path. Failure should be applauded, not condemned, but it must be learned from.

To go exponential, you need to embed the operational, tactical and strategic states until this approach is well honed. Then you will be in the place to start thinking about the final stage – the true intent of the 10×Generation state.

Taking your vision to the stars, breaking free of the atmosphere, and propelling your team into orbit and beyond. When you are all invested in the same vision, have streamlined your processes, have alignment at every level, going exponential is the logical next stage.

So, what's stopping you?

How do I know if this guide is for me?

This guide is for you if you work in any organization that is not meeting its objectives; where there is friction between teams, a lack of visibility between departments, and constant change programmes that lead to little or nothing in the way of tangible outcomes. Each role in an organization should have a voice and be able to have a positive impact on the organization's success. In the 10×Generation state, this is possible from the most junior to the most senior role.

This guide is for you if have a role in the operational view, for example:

- You are a head of technology – who isn't sure why there needs to be another change
- You are a leader who wants to create more leaders and not managers
- You are a technical lead who constantly feels that they are left in the dark when critical decisions are made about the technology you use
- You are working in technology, though not necessarily in a lead or management role, but you want visibility of what is happening in your organization
- You are a solution architect who is a decision maker, but feel that you are not being heard and are hamstrung in making the best decisions based on your capabilities
- You have just started in a small startup or scaleup and want to bring maturity and visibility to the organization
- You are working in a small-to-medium business and have experienced bloat first-hand, where there are a lot of roles but there is uncertainty about what each role's function is
- You are an experienced IT leader but have little or no visibility into the workings of other departments.

This guide is for you if have a role in the tactical view, for example:

- You are a department head having change thrust upon you without a clear understanding of the necessity of the change
- You are a department head with little or no visibility of what is important to other departments
- You are a department head with little understanding of the organization's strategy and how this links in with your department
- You are a department lead (including, but not limited to, heads of finance, people and culture, sales and marketing, and customer service) who has responsibility but is not able to make the best decisions for the organization

- You are working in a department, though not necessarily in a lead or management role, but you want visibility of what is happening in your organization
- You lead a team but are constantly challenged by upper leadership when you are trying to make decisions that affect your team.

This guide is for you if have a role in the strategic view, for example:

- You are a chief executive officer (CEO) or chief financial officer (CFO) who needs to reduce costs and continue to deliver with the same or less headcount
- You are a CEO facing a lack of diversity at the senior level of your organization
- You are a CEO who is facing a lack of key leadership successors
- You are a CEO who has been recommended digital transformations multiple times, only to find that every one of them fails to deliver the results promised
- You are a CEO of a startup who used brute force to achieve outcomes, but are now embarking on the next stage of growth and are unsure how to do this
- You are the CEO of a scaleup needing to grow, but are experiencing significant bloating of processes and people
- You are a CEO who wants to understand how to have a fault-tolerant organization
- You are a chief technology officer (CTO) who is about to start in a new mid-sized organization that has had rapid growth
- You are a CTO who wants to have a flat organization structure that can scale without losing efficiencies
- You are a CTO or chief information officer (CIO) who wants to be successful in their first 30, 60 or 90 days
- You are a CTO joining a new business and do not want to make the same mistakes as your predecessor
- You are a CTO fighting to recruit or retain top talent
- You are a CFO who wants to understand what IT does, and you do not understand digital transformation
- You are a CIO or CTO struggling to successfully bridge the gap between IT and the senior executive or board
- You are working in a support function such as executive assistant, and you want visibility of what is happening in your organization
- You are a chief marketing officer (CMO) trying to navigate the changing landscape of digital marketing and customer engagement
- You are a chief human resources officer (CHRO) looking to foster a more collaborative and engaged workplace
- You are a chief customer officer (CCO) seeking ways to enhance customer satisfaction and loyalty
- You are a chief data officer (CDO) aiming to leverage data for strategic decision-making.

Acknowledgements

The authors would like to thank the following people for their generosity in helping bring this publication to life.

Shane Baldacchino, for his continuing support of the authors during the writing process. For providing wonderful praise for the book and for understanding the need for change in a changing and challenging environment.

Jodie Coomer, for her endless energy, reading and re-reading every iteration of the guide – always offering solid, constructive advice while keeping the authors on track. For never losing interest, and picking up all those tiny grammatical errors that so often get overlooked.

Jane Hoban, for providing her expertise from a marketing and trading perspective. For giving freely of her time and enabling the authors to view MarTech from a business perspective. It takes a lot of time to review a book and write constructive feedback, and the authors are truly grateful.

Craig Howe, for agreeing to review the text during his incredibly busy schedule. The authors are grateful to him in so many ways: for being a wonderful human being and one of our greatest supporters; for taking the time to workshop some of the heavier concepts; and for challenging our thinking. The value of this support cannot be underestimated.

Alex Louey, for providing invaluable experience as the CEO of a startup that has rapidly grown to a scaleup and beyond. For letting the authors pick his brain in understanding the pitfalls of the startup culture.

Graham Padgham, for being part of the review process even though he was in the midst of a new role. This willingness to take the time to review our work is truly appreciated.

Ben Spera, for providing vital feedback on the book from the start of the reviewing process. Without this valuable insight from our peers, it would not have been possible to write a book that meets the needs of all organizations.

Tim Wyatt, for agreeing to and taking the time to review a manuscript from an ex-colleague of Mary-Beth who was in need of his expertise. From one colleague across the pond in Australia to another in the UK, thank you so much.

The team at TSO, for taking a punt on two authors determined to shake up the status quo in organizational design, and for believing in this publication and its power to change the way businesses operate.

Personal thanks

Ady Kalra extends his heartfelt gratitude to **Anna Edwards**, not only for her unwavering support during his absence but also for her exceptional care in nurturing their little one, Indus.

Mary-Beth Hosking would like to thank **Stuart Hosking** for always being there and for being her biggest advocate, and **Jackson Hosking**, for being her rock when things have felt hopeless.

Acknowledgements from TSO

We would like to give special thanks to the team of experts who provided valuable feedback during content development. Their time and effort to do this are greatly appreciated. A big thankyou to Jodie Coomer, Jane Hoban, Valence Howden, Craig Howe, NJ Robinson, Ben Spera and Tim Wyatt.

1 Introduction

In the last decade, with the advent of multiple delivery frameworks, organizations have been investing substantial funding into pivoting to new ways of working in an attempt to get their product or service out to the customer as soon as possible.

The most common reasons for these pivots are to ensure parity with competition, to have a unique selling point, and to satisfy the executive and board members.[3] There has been a huge shift in how organizations are structured, how software is delivered and the growing need for everyone in the business to understand technology.

What most chief executive officers (CEOs) are looking for is a business that is future-proofed. What that really implies is flexibility, but it also alludes to speed to market. This leads to a shift in mindset and an organizational overhaul. Ultimately this organizational change ends up being the buzzword we are all familiar with: *digital transformation.*

Efficiencies lost

When organizational leaders think about efficiencies, their focus will be at the operational layer and will generally lead to technology being thought of as the main cause. The crux of the problem is a disconnect between the strategic imperative to improve overall efficiencies and a fundamental understanding of the operational layer's needs to ensure smooth delivery. This culminates in a lack of visibility of outcomes across all layers of the organization – but, as technology is the most visible, and one of the biggest lines in the CFO's budget forecast, this is where assumptions on rectifying the situation are made.

This leads organizations to conclude that bringing in a new technology leader or external consultants to address the lack of agility and underperformance will solve the problem. If you have been with the organization for an extended period, or have seen the company grow from a startup to mid-size, you will be familiar with the infinite loop of change failures experienced (see Figure 2 for the 'wheel of chaos').

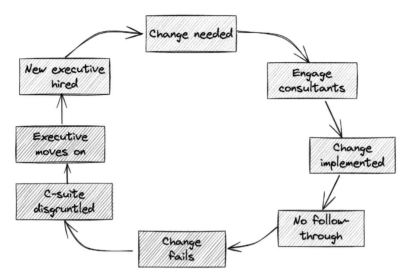

Figure 2 The wheel of chaos

The executive leadership (or above) will acknowledge that a change is needed. This is why it was brought on board in the first place: to fix the issues with ever-waning delivery that the CEO sees, and the ever-increasing technology costs that the CFO is unhappy with.

The CIO or equivalent executive will engage consultants to review the organizational structure. The consultants will suggest a digital transformation project to fix the problems the organization is experiencing. The term 'digital transformation' is vague in its nature, as it can relate to many things, and generally no one is quite sure what it actually means. If there is a lack of alignment with the problem being addressed, the scope tends to be challenging to deliver. Of course, this proposal makes absolute sense to senior leadership, as, anecdotally, the problems experienced are seen to be with the IT-focused product and technology teams – so why not bring in the experts in to fix them?

In general, however, the consultants will focus on only a few roles in the operational tier, doing one of two things:

- In the product and technology functions, they will narrowly focus on working with the product managers and engineering leadership, and will ignore the other roles across this tier who make the function operate
- They will be more expansive in their approach, but still limited to working with product managers, engineers, architecture and IT operations (some roles are still ignored).

Limiting the roles and teams to engage with will lead to an entire subset of activities being missed, including (but not limited to):

- Customer service
- The voice of the customer
- IT operations, and how any change will affect the day-to-day running of the organization
- Cost of change, and how this impedes the HR function and impacts staff retention
- Finance teams, and how the transformation will disrupt financial costs and processing
- Advocacy, public relations, marketing and communications.

Yet another digital transformation

As yet another digital transformation progresses, the consultants will have key deliverables that they must adhere to. Once these have been met, the consultants will promise that the organization will become much more profitable and achieve higher market evaluations.

According to the MIT Center for Digital Business, 'Companies that have embraced digital transformation are 26% more profitable than their average industry competitors and enjoy a 12% higher market valuation.'[4] This increase in profitability is what the executive leadership is hoping for, and it will see this baseline percentage as a starting point.

Although most executives have clear goals to achieve via the digital transformation, most don't understand technology and are naïve on key measures of success. There is a lack of governance, and little importance is placed on driving the initiatives towards the organizational goals. They don't align on key terms and vision – there usually isn't a clearly defined 'North Star'. Usually there is some alignment between the executive and the board. The board tends to hire the members of the exec on their vision and experience. However, there can be substantial gaps in translating that into senior management and others executing on that vision.

This leaves the business and leadership with gaps across the teams that have not seen any positive effect from the transformation. The teams in the various departments that are excluded from the digital transformation will have little or no visibility of the change, and will not see many positive impacts from it. The ways of working, the systems impact and the potential staffing changes will destabilize, and create division between, the operational tier and the organization's departments.

It is at this point that many digital transformations fail, as shown in Figure 3.

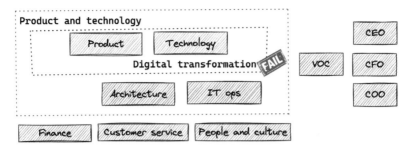

Figure 3 Yet another digital transformation where only product and technology are considered

VOC = Voice of the customer, which bridges the gap between product and technology and the C-suite executives

When the change fails, the executives are disappointed. The cost of change to the organization will be substantial, and the lack of outputs will create even greater pressure on the operational tier. Many team members in this space may also be thrust into the digital transformation project under the remit of the project management office. When the change fails, they feel a sense of responsibility; many who have not been adequately engaged also feel disempowered, and are unlikely to embrace the transformation.

At this point the individual executive who was responsible for making the decision will potentially move on from the business, having delivered a change that was unsuccessful, only to embark on another digital transformation that is much needed in another organization. If they choose not to move on, they are then lumbered with an inefficient operating model and will recommend another project with changed scope – which, in disguise, is yet another digital transformation with its very own code name.

If a new executive is hired to deliver yet another digital transformation, the organization will most likely go back to the old ways of working.

What went wrong?

For most digital transformations, there is a misunderstanding that only the digital layer is affected. It makes perfect sense that the main area for poor performance should be the only area of focus. However, as with any blockage, once one area is unblocked, the flow-on will impact somewhere else. The same can be said for an organization. If you focus only on one area and forget the rest, eventually the impacts will be felt downstream and upstream.

If you do not take a holistic view of your organization, any transformation is destined for failure. To understand your organization, it is important to understand the path already taken, and what is seen as important from the top down and the bottom up.

When a startup is formed, there is a sense of eagerness to pitch a product idea and seek funding. The team in this organization is prepared to undertake any role and do what is needed to get a minimal viable product out of the door to satisfy potential investors. The output is significant, and all areas of the business communicate with each other to achieve a common goal. The startup is an exciting place to work, and isn't bogged down with unnecessary processes. It is messy and frantic, but in among this disorder, the outputs are high. The culture places people and the customer first, which manifests into free-flowing ideas and everyone being on a common journey to achieve outcomes.

This is the true essence of the 10×Generation, where the business thrives on agility and adaptability. It is a place of curiosity, not hesitancy: without a lot of existing burdensome systems there are more 'greenfields' to explore, as opposed to a potential need to 'challenge the status quo' and deal with the impending politics that arise.

Not Another Digital Transformation is not a digital transformation guide – it is an organizational alignment guide, and will provide advice to help you achieve this state.

To scale or not to scale

When a startup transitions into the next phase of organizational evolution, it will begin to scale. This is primarily because the frantic nature of a startup is not sustainable, and some structure is needed. The question that needs an answer is: 'How do we scale the mindset?'

As the organization begins to scale, the first thing that is noticed is a downturn in efficiencies compared with the startup stage. This is a by-product of several scenarios:

- Bringing in new employees who want to bring their old ways of working from their previous employment with them. There is a 'This is how we did it back in X, so we should do that here' type of thinking
- Premature scaling and not having a plan for holistic outcomes
- Conflict of interest on vision among C-suite and founders
- New leaders chasing new shiny opportunities without gaining command on existing organizational challenges
- Eventually 'Culture starts eating strategy for breakfast'.

Over time, as hierarchies are formed, processes are implemented and human capital is employed, additional complexities compound on the operational layer, slowing down the pace of delivery. For many executives or founders, this is seen as a cost of growth, when it shouldn't be. The impacts to the business are absorbed, and the business keeps growing while costs increase, the workforce grows, processes get more and more muddy, and ultimately delivery lessens.

As shown in Figure 4, the expectation and the reality are poles apart, and sometimes the expectation is unrealistic. The executives believe that as the company matures and they have more budget to scale the organization, the velocity should increase, when the opposite is actually the case. The organization's structure impedes agility, and is the first place to look for answers to the problem. Instead of focusing on a single view, executives need to broaden their mindset, and take in all organizational views at once – this will highlight the interfaces between views, and show where the bottlenecks are forming.

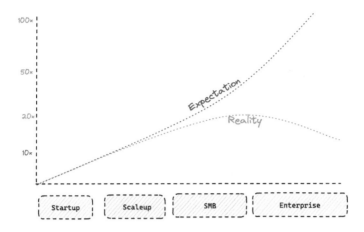

Figure 4 The expectation vs reality conundrum

10×Generation views

To understand the operational, tactical and strategic views at greater length, we need to zoom out and look at organization management. If we ascend to a 30,000-foot view of organizational awareness, we will see that all businesses can be broken down into three layers. These are similar to the levels referred to in the US Armed Forces' doctrine of warfare: strategic, operational and tactical, where tactical actions link to national objectives.

There are no finite limits or boundaries between these levels, but they help commanders design and synchronize operations, allocate resources and assign tasks to the appropriate command layer. The strategic, operational or tactical purpose of employment depends on the nature of the objective, mission or task.[5]

The roles linked with each view are shown in Figure 5. This publication will reference the strategic view from the lens of a C-suite executive: the tactical view is aligned with different departments' goals, and the operational view is the engine where product is engineered and the technology decisions related to the product are made.

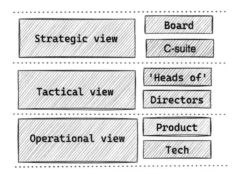

Figure 5 Roles linked with each view

Figure 6 gives a perspective on the growth journey from the operational, tactical and strategic views of a startup, scaleup, small-to-medium business (SMB) and enterprise. It provides a view of the type of organization you may be working in and the challenges you may face.

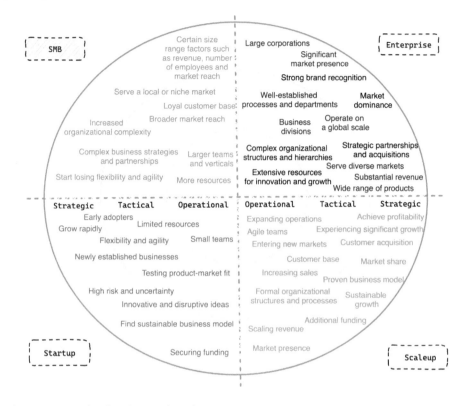

Figure 6 Organizational growth radar

Startup – private-sector organization with fewer than 50 employees

Scaleup – private-sector organization between startup and SMB: 50 to 500 employees

SMB (small to medium business) – private-sector organization with fewer than 1000 (or 500 to 999) employees

Enterprise – any public-sector organization, or a private-sector organization with 1000 or more employees

2 Boarding: The operational view

The operational view (or operational layer) is the foundation layer in any organization, and for the purposes of this publication will represent the product and technology teams – better known as the 'IT folk'.* This is where product-driven technology decisions are made and implemented. The operational view of product and technology is the engine room in any business, whatever type of industry it supports. When something goes wrong with any aspect of the technology in your organization, this is where you will hear 'That's IT's fault.' IT represents everything technologically related, and as such is the bedrock when we discuss the operational view.

The team members who work in this layer may vary from business to business, as will the structure of the IT department, but in essence they are product and technology-focused individuals, and will provide the support needed to ensure continuous delivery. We will now look at the operational state for all organizational types from the view of a startup, scaleup, SMB and enterprise.

Startup

In a startup,[6] the operation will be lean in nature and will consist of purely product and technology team members and a founder. At times a startup will have one or more founders who build the core of the business first. Generally they will wear many hats at the beginning, eventually handing these responsibilities over to others as part of the scaling process.

These team members will work across multiple disciplines to deliver rapidly to the business. The purpose of a startup is to get product built and into 'the wild' to see whether it gains traction either as a standalone product or service, or as a new feature

---

* Not all organizations are product-based, but they all will have an IT function.

set sold in support of a primary product. The structure of the operational view in a startup is flat, and all team members will work autonomously to deliver rapidly to the business. There is little friction as teams work towards a shared vision.

There is a sense of urgency and excitement in a startup that is unsustainable in the long term, but the culture and agility that it fosters brings a group of disparate individuals together and focuses their energy on a single objective. When the mix is right, this creates an experience that is hard to replicate as an organization begins to scale.

In a startup, the operational world is a place where no one feels underappreciated. By necessity, everyone wears many hats, giving the organization and individuals the advantage of being close to the business needs. The startup works as a single unit with a strong sense of purpose, and defines the potential of product and technology as a cohesive entity.

In the successful startup, the product and technology roles that are employed in the beginning will transition to the scaleup and take on greater duties and responsibilities. The 'jack of all trades' mentality needs to transform into specialists leading different areas of the business as the organization scales. This is the next logical step in the organization's evolution, and is the place where the efficiency gains of the startup are impacted and start a slow decline.

The operational view

The power of the operational view in a startup is that it always has access to the corresponding strategic view with a close relationship to the founders of the organization.

Scaleup

In a scaleup, the operational view will start to take shape. To manage the influx of more personnel, there will need to be more lead-level roles providing additional structure to the organization. During this stage, many scaleups will be burdened by additional processes and governance, and extensive resources.

The question that needs to be answered is: 'Will your startup ever be prosperous enough to scale up, and if it does, what is needed to transition successfully?'

Assuming your startup is ready to scale up, new people will be employed to help manage the transition, providing greater leadership and maturity to the business. What usually happens, however, is that people who are brought in will 'lift and shift' their old ways of working, where they had additional levels of support, and supplant them into the scaleup.

When this happens, the slow transition away from a lean, productive company will begin – but, as with the boiled frog analogy, this happens so slowly that it goes unnoticed until it's too late. The problem is caused by the type of mindset of the individuals hired, which sets the tone going forward. New hires are meant to represent the continuation of the vision and modern practices that have supported the business to this point. As the scaleup matures and continues to deliver, at a slower rate than the startup, the founder and the product and technology teams will justify the slowdown as a by-product of greater governance, which is a direct reflection of hiring practices.

This is also where the divide between the people who started in the organization during the startup phase and the new people who have joined will grow.

The shift also may occur when an organization has more 'skin in the game': more products out in the wild that it needs to protect rather than create. This shift requires additional stabilizing practices, but this cannot be at the expense of productivity.

The reduction in delivery will become an accepted outcome of the scaling process, and the organization will continue to grow into an SMB with the old ways of working becoming bedded in and hard to change.

SMB

In an SMB, the operational view will start displaying additional headcount with 'head of' roles. The 'head of' roles in the operational layer will be brought on board, or promoted from those who have been in the company during the startup or scaleup stage. Even greater levels of governance and processes will be introduced.

The justification for these roles will include additional governance and cost management, and improvement of declining delivery output. There will also be discussion of a reduction in debt* (both technical and organizational) that may have accumulated in the earlier stages of growth. As with many SMBs, addressing the debt will not be a cost that can be accommodated, and this will potentially be kicked down the road as the business continues to grow. As the debt accrues, it increases the organization's risk profile and will eventually have a huge impact from a cost and stability perspective.

The growth phase of an SMB is where the real trouble begins. Budgets need to be adhered to, and cost-saving measures are employed to reduce the deficiencies of an inept scaling process. While costs have increased, delivery has gone down from when the business started and funding was secured.

The organization will look for cost savings and budget reductions as a way to compensate for the lack of delivery and inflated headcounts. This short-sighted view will drive behaviours that, from the outside, do not appear conducive to the organization's success.

Leaders in the operational view will start hoarding budgets, shying away from opportunities to improve efficiency and reduce technical debt. This will be driven by a fear of losing budget in the next budgeting round. The double-edged sword of the leadership in the operational view is one of 'simple mathematics'. If I save money by making the technology more efficient, I want to use this saving for innovation. However, what actually happens is that the cost savings are then removed from the next year's

---

* Organizational debt relates to all of the people and process compromises that were made as the organization scaled, which create a burden on efficiencies.

budget, and therefore no innovation takes place. This way of operating results in an industry-wide behaviour in which leaders do not want to repeat the same mistake in the next organization they work in, and thus budget-hoarding begins.

During this stage, the founder is no longer at the coalface and has lost all visibility of the actions taking place in the operational layer. Decisions will be made that impact overall efficiencies, and the SMB leadership will no longer have a way of countering the efficiency losses without adding more human capital.

As the organization continues to grow, the delivery is significantly lowered; process and technical debt continues to rise, with no clear path to address it; and the levels of human capital, processes and governance are almost crippling. At no time in the SMB, scaleup or startup is the voice of the customer (VOC) a consideration: in fact, in most companies there is no VOC.

This is when the saying 'Do the culture before it does you' makes most sense. You want to make sure that the culture you build from startup to scaleup transforms in the best way to support the SMB.

Enterprise

In an enterprise, the operational view will incorporate the VOC role, as this is a common role implemented by most C-suite operational leaders. The VOC role is one of the more important ones in the organization, as it enables the operational layer to take into consideration what the customer actually wants from the organization's products and services.

Similarly to an SMB, the enterprise will have multiple leadership roles depending on the organizational structure that has been adopted. Generally, the larger the organization becomes, the more hierarchical it will be. This structure will reduce visibility for those working in the operational layer, and will create greater friction points. The more friction points, the greater the impact on the organization's ability to deliver. It is at the enterprise level that the organization has flipped the pyramid of efficiencies and has reached its newest delivery low.

At this stage, most enterprises have a lot to lose: reputational damage cannot be taken lightly. If the enterprise is making money, that creates further challenges at the operational layer. A common maxim used by leadership is 'If it ain't broke, don't fix it.' This thinking creates a dripping-tap effect, meaning that no one cares about an issue until it becomes a tangible one that impacts the organization. When this happens, it leads to a complete overhaul or rewrite of systems and processes, or – you guessed it! …

YADT – 'yet another digital transformation'.

3 Take-off: The tactical view

The tactical view or tactical layer is the glue that binds together different departments of any organization. For the purposes of this publication, in any business, it will represent all departments that have senior leadership who report into the C-suite.

The team members who work in this layer may vary from business to business, but in essence they are in clusters of teams focused on departmental objectives, and will have both inputs to and outputs from the operational layer. In the warfare model referenced in Chapter 1, this is generally where the tactical response is initiated. We will now look at the tactical state for all organizational types from the view of a startup, scaleup, SMB and enterprise.

Startup

In a startup organization, the tactical view generally does not exist in the way it does in larger, more mature organizations, because of its flat structure. Departmental activities are undertaken by team members working in the operational layer. The presence of many hats removes friction and fosters open communication. It also increases speed to market, and creates time and space to generate new ideas. The disadvantages, though, are the lack of specialized skills, confusion about ownership and an inability to scale.

Scaleup

In a scaleup organization, the tactical layer begins to emerge. Departments start to form, with groups of experts separated by specialization and/or location.

Generally, one of the first areas to scale should be the people and culture (P&C) team, previously known as 'human resources' (HR). This represents internally facing processes, and resource governance that is brought into the business under the guidance of P&C and finance. Externally facing processes are introduced by customer service, marketing, sales and legal.

The scaleup has fewer friction points, as the organization is still learning and growing.[7] Without a clear path to the desired organizational design, more headcount is added and departments grow in silos.

In the scaleup, the tactical layer will be an immature function, but will start adding levels of governance that are needed to navigate some of the complexities that will become present in the organization. With additional funding and pressures to meet expected deliverables, the scaleup will start to experience growing pains that could be circumvented with a structural growth strategy. Most companies feel the pressure of not growing as fast year-on-year as they scale, and this has a flow-on effect on the need to add more people.

Like all companies working on growth strategies, whether that be organic or inorganic, the focus will be on how to attain profitability. This route to profitability will focus on delivery outcomes, cost-control measures, increased governance and market pressures, and expansion. At no point will there be a clear focus on the organizational structure and how this will grow with the organization. If there is a focus, it will be old thinking, with a tall organizational structure with additional management layers to ensure a level of control is imposed on the growing organization.

SMB

In an SMB organization, the tactical view will show significant signs of organizational growth. The middle-management tier will have multiple levels of hierarchy. The flat structure of the startup organization will be overrun by the hierarchies needed to support a tall structure. The justification of this growth will be to ensure greater governance in an effort to create clear lines of communication, enable escalation to take place, and give senior decision makers the opportunity to guide the strategic direction of the organization.

At a minimum, the SMB will have directors or 'head of' roles supporting finance, customer service, and people and culture (P&C). The management roles in the scaleup will report into the 'head of' roles, with the intent to provide greater structure; however, if we return to the purpose of governance (which is to influence how an organization's objectives are set and achieved, how risk is monitored and addressed, and how performance is optimized), this additional layering is not the best way to achieve this as it introduces greater complexity and reduces visibility across the layers.

Enterprise

In the enterprise organization, the tactical view will be similar to that of the SMB. Additional headcount will be employed in departments to support the increasing growth of the organization. This will be justified by the thinking that additional bureaucracy and decision points across the layers are needed to support the growing need at an enterprise level. Friction between the operational and tactical view will be extremely high, and additional business-partnering-type roles will be brought on to increase visibility and smooth communications.

This process creates more divisions within each of the operational, tactical and strategic layers in the overarching tactical view. By zooming into each layer, you will see that each has its own concept of operational, tactical and strategic views (see Figure 7). This is necessary in order for the layers to function, and it will carry on as growth continues. This nesting of layers creates friction points as more layers of governance are implemented.

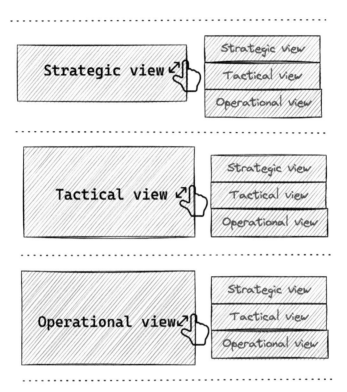

Figure 7 Layer within layer. Each view has its own operational, tactical and strategic layers

4 Cruising: The strategic view

The strategic view or strategic layer represents the executive layer in an organization. It includes the C-suite executives, whose primary role is that of strategic decision-making. In a standard pyramid structure, this is the part at the top.

The executives in this layer will vary depending on the size and type of organization. They will take the information provided by the tactical layer and use it to make informed decisions about the strategic direction of the organization. We will now look at the strategic state for all organizational types from the view of a startup, scaleup, SMB and enterprise.

Startup

In a startup organization, the strategic view resides purely in the operational view. The founder will support from within the operational layer, and will guide the strategic direction of the organization from the operational view.

Scaleup

In a scaleup organization, the strategic view will include a CEO. It may also include the founder if they choose to be in that layer. Alternatively, the founder may remain at the operational layer, enabling them to stay in the organization's engine room, guiding delivery from the product and technology space. The communication between the CEO and founder is achieved by setting clearly defined expectations when the executive is onboarded. This ensures that the founder still has a direct line of sight to the CEO, and input into the vision for the organization.

If the founder continues in the strategic layer, communication between the CEO and founder is even more important to prevent friction points being created.

The reason why scaleups bring in a CEO at this stage is to provide the governance needed to manage with the hurdles presented by venture capital funding, and to ensure that a clear growth strategy is considered. If the organization is aiming to be included on a regional or global stock exchange, there will need to be someone with a proven track record to guide it on this path.

With a CEO in place, there will now be a solid disconnect between the operational and strategic views. Unless there is a seasoned CEO who understands the function of the operational engine room, this is where the first instances of friction between the layers will be felt.

It is at this stage that it is important for the three layers to work well together and have little or no friction. However, this is generally where friction is observed and will continue as the organization grows.

SMB

In an SMB organization, the bloat is well entrenched and there will be many friction points. The CEO, the CFO and the founder will now be residing at the strategic level. The founder will no longer be driving the engine room, and their voice will be reduced between the layers.

It is at this stage in an SMB where founders may leave the organization because their voice is no longer the driving force for its direction. Without the original direction from the founders, this is where many SMB organizations falter, key staff members resign and intellectual property walks out of the door.

Additional C-suite roles are employed to manage with the increasing compliance needs. If the organization's SMB has been included on its country's stock exchange (such as ASX or NASDAQ), additional reporting and compliance is required, and there needs to be a CFO.

Enterprise

In the enterprise organization, as it continues to grow, additional headcount will be employed and there will be operational impacts. As the product delivery slows to the lowest yet, and there is greater contention across all layers of the enterprise, another C-suite team member will need to be brought in to improve the enterprise's operational efficiencies. The role of chief operating officer (COO) will be introduced to fix the organization's waning delivery, with the intent of creating greater visibility for the CEO.

At this point, the bloat is out of control. Additional C-suite heads will eventually filter down to all other tiers with greater management layering, in an attempt to improve the organization's delivery. If the organization is impeded by legacy systems, the recommendation will once again lead to the same conclusion: *YADT*.

From startup to enterprise (see Figure 8), many decisions are made to increase the organization's productivity without a clearly defined organizational strategy. When the startup begins, the intent is to survive to the next reporting cycle, get funding and grow. Survival lends itself to a way of thinking that is not sustainable in the long term.

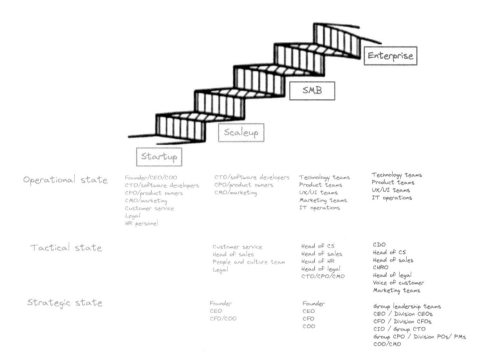

Figure 8 Steps of growth

However, at no point on the path from startup to scaleup to SMB to enterprise do we see a concerted effort to clearly define how the organization should be structured for success. We see old thinking and old ways of responding to market pressures. More headcount, more management and control, which causes silos and bloat, and impedes the organization's ability to respond rapidly.

If the organization survives to the next step in its evolution, there is a sense that it may be too late to change the structure – but it seems that it is never too late to undertake a digital transformation.

Next steps

No matter where you are in your organization's evolution, the important thing to know is that it is not too late to review your organization's structure and embrace 10×Generation thinking.

In the following chapters, we will take you through the myriad of problems faced across organizations and how they can address these by using 10×Generation thinking. By embracing a prosperous mindset and opening yourself up to a different way of operating, no matter which level you are in and no matter where you are in your organization's expansion aspirations, you will be able to achieve sustainable growth and tap back into the achievements experienced during the heady days of a startup.

5 The 10×Generation

During the last 20 years or so, as technology companies have become major global powers in their own right, many books have been written about organizational design and the best way to achieve maximum output in the technology space. We are all familiar with the Agile Manifesto,[8] the Phoenix and Unicorn Project, and the benefits of DevOps[9] and the extension to DevSecOps.[10] All have an aim of ensuring greater agility and removing the burdensome overhead that the waterfall methodology[11] has created, by trying to address reductions in productivity.

An organization will use multiple internal frameworks to support departmental needs, including people and culture (P&C) approaches to joiners, movers and leavers, managing teams etc.; finance approaches for consolidations and financial close-out timings; and a myriad of others. Each framework will be designed to provide a standard that everyone can work to.

Whichever framework is used, the common denominator is that it relies on, or interfaces with, technology in some way. This interaction is therefore seen as the cause of declining productivity, and the technology department is believed to be to blame. It can be argued that this makes absolute sense if the organization is a technology company – it is technology, right? The issue with this singular approach is that, regardless of whether an organization is a technology company, it will still include various layers and frameworks. If you focus purely on the technology department, you are missing the other layers and levels of interaction needed to bring cohesion across departments. This lack of visibility and alignment will make the difference between a successful and an unsuccessful transformation.

As we saw in the preface, the 10×Generation is a method by which an organization can achieve exponential growth while maintaining the same level of autonomy, visibility and alignment as enjoyed in a startup environment. Each view has the same visibility within its own layers as it does of each adjoining view. In essence, lines of communication are open within each view and across all of them. There is an explicit understanding of the operational, tactical and strategic layers, both across and within. Alignment is reached as all layers are inextricably linked across the entire organization (see Figure 9).

Figure 9 The 10×Generation relationships
All views impact each other and must work cohesively

As an example, the operational view would have a product and technology strategy with individual roadmaps that various layers in the organization need to execute. This could be the strategy of the product and technology department, but it's important that this strategy is aligned with all other departments and there is cross-pollination of the various strategies at play.

It is, therefore, not just about digital transformation – it's an *organizational* transformation that's really needed. Performing a digital transformation is like changing the wheels of a car and expecting it to go faster.

You may be thinking that you have already linked your organization's strategy across all levels, but is this really the case? Different layers will have different strategies, but they will all ultimately link to the organization's overarching strategic intent. Without each layer having its own identity within the whole, and an understanding of how its identity impacts the others, there is no alignment.

The 10×Generation: A winning method

The 10×Generation is the way in which you will organize yourselves to gain maximum visibility, velocity and alignment in your organization.

The challenges

There are three key challenges that impact and drive behaviours across all organizations, regardless of their size, maturity or industry. By addressing these, you will make the greatest possible impact in shifting the dial towards the 10×Generation state. Within each layer – operational, tactical or strategic – the challenges will be brought to life when you look at the various scenarios that may be taking place for you right now.

The list of scenarios presented is not exhaustive, but will generate enough ideas to help you to iterate and make changes that will shift your organization from its current design to the 10×Generation state.

When researching the scenarios for this publication, we kept coming across the same issues:

- Misalignment of the organization's structure
- Digital transformation being seen as the only alternative to poor performance
- Silos among departments from startup or scaleup to enterprise, which worsens when you go from local to global.

Misalignment of the organization's structure

For many organizations, this is where all the main problems will stem from. There will be different structures throughout the organization, different ways of working and a lack of visibility at every layer, increasing drag. It is here where the organization will experience significant bloat as it adds more layers of management to deal with increasing barriers to delivery.

Friction points are many, but can be broken down into the following:

- Non-existent or limited visibility between departments
- Lack of knowledge of the ways of working in different departments, which increases wastage[12] across the organization
- Multiple layers of management to control the work being performed, and lack of alignment between management layers
- Multiple layers and more administration, creating an increasingly bloated organization
- Management controlling accountability, with a lack of empowerment to the lower levels in the structure.

Many leaders will understand this challenge, and many have already recognized that if they grow their organization too fast and do not align the structure to support the people in it, there will eventually be only two possible courses of action: to transform or to start again.[13]

Transforming or starting again may mean a complete overhaul of the organization, considerable downsizing or the organization's eventual demise.

What is waste?

Many organizations, regardless of size or position in their growth trajectory, will begin experiencing wastage and bloat. To understand what this means in the 10×Generation, it is useful to look at the Lean Six Sigma concepts of waste and how they are applied. As we are focusing on digital transformation and organizations that are impacted by it, not all of the waste elements are applicable. Waste at a glance:[14]

- **Transportation** The unnecessary moving around of material, people and equipment
- **Inventory** Excessive inventory that takes up valuable space, management and capital
- **Motion** Unnecessary and dangerous movement that can harm people
- **Waiting** The time wasted waiting for people, equipment, materials and information to arrive
- **Overproduction** Producing more than the customer or your process needs
- **Overprocessing** Doing more than the customer wants, needs or is willing to pay for
- **Defects** The production of a defective product or delivery of service, resulting in rework
- **Skills** Not using people's talent, knowledge and experience to improve the organization.

Digital transformation – the only alternative

When an organization determines that it cannot successfully scale and continue to deliver value to its customer, and is losing market share, only one alternative will be presented – digital transformation – when there are potentially other options. A digital transformation can mean many things: a shift to digital delivery of products and services, new approaches to what is provided, or simply a shift to cloud services. However, we are focusing on *large-scale* digital transformations that focus on the technology department and how it interfaces with the rest of an organization. This is discussed at the beginning of this publication, and is a key area that has seldom been successfully addressed.

There are only a few case studies where full alignment across the entire organization has enabled a full digital transformation to take place. This is due to a visionary few who realized that there was a better way.[15] The focus needs to be broader than one layer of the organization – it must be across all layers. Buy-in must be achieved from every person in the organization, otherwise the transformation will fail.

On a global scale, the digital transformation is the go-to option to address poor performance, scalability and supportability in an organization. Digital transformations are also among the most poorly understood actions that are undertaken. This view is supported by many leaders and consultants who do not have an alternative approach to provide. If the focus is on the technology layer, the scope is much smaller, which may be why the approach has never been extended beyond that of the traditional technology or operational view.

Silos worsen from local to global

Finally, when an organization does not have a strategic view supported by consistent and known ways of working to support across teams and departments, we see silos forming. As the organization grows and moves from a local business to a global one, the problem deepens, and the lack of productivity between departments eventually impacts the organization's overall productivity. This will lead to an 'us versus them' culture and create friction points.

Silos can be seen as a by-product of the misaligned organization, one where rate of change, culture and management are significantly underdeveloped.[16] However, it goes further than this. Silos can be formed when, culturally, the needs of the organization's individual departments are not considered to be as important as its overall objectives, leading to a misalignment of strategy. There is a lack of understanding in the departmental layer that aligns with the organization's overall goals. Silos can also be formed when the organization has a 'go to market' need, and a division is formed around a specific capability or offering. This newly formed group thinks it has everything the customer needs to execute in its space.

Within the silo, we will see a culture that affects everyone within and outside of the silo. Friction points from a silo-driven organization will have the following features:

- Obstructive culture makes it challenging for departments to engage with team members in the silo
- Work objectives external to the silo are de-prioritized within it, and this impacts cross-functional work objectives
- Leadership in the silo creates performance objectives that are not aligned with, and operate at cross-purposes to, the overall organization's strategy
- Having objectives in conflict with overall strategic intent will lead to individuals behaving based on inappropriate objectives, causing significant clashes
- Escalations are not addressed cross-functionally but higher up, creating agitation between management layers, which impacts productivity.

From a workforce perspective, we will see employee dissatisfaction, as resistance across teams impacts the ability of individuals and departments to do their jobs effectively.

Each challenge is explored in this publication via the use of conversations between personas that exist in most organizations of these types. You may have experienced such a conversation in your past. In Chapter 7, the conversations are represented as scripts from a play, to help build on the ambience of the moment that the conversation took place.

If you cannot wait to read the scripts, jump to Chapter 7.

6 The 10×Generation principles

Now that we have clearly defined the challenges that most organizations face, the next step is to understand the principles that will provide the differentiation between the current state and the 10×Generation state.

Each principle has a number of elements that need to be implemented to ensure that the full force of the principle is embedded in the organization. Each element is as important as the next and cannot be dismissed when looking to transform the organization.

The 10×Generation principles, as depicted in Figure 10, can be abbreviated to EA^3: empowerment, adaptation, assessment and alignment.

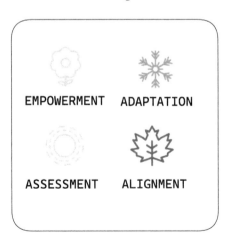

Figure 10 The 10×Generation principles – EA³

First principle: Empowerment

Empowerment is the first principle in the 10×Generation state, and is the foundation layer. It is broken down into three elements (see Figure 11). Each is as important as the other, and they can be addressed in any order, provided that they are embedded before moving on to the next layer. Each individual in the organization must understand the importance of this first principle and embrace it. This will determine the success or failure of your transition to the 10×Generation state.

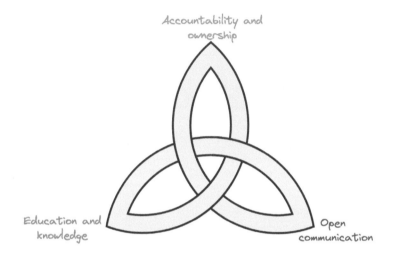

Figure 11 Empowerment Venn. All elements interlink and are necessary for success

Accountability and ownership

Each individual in the organization understands their role in it: what they are responsible for and what they directly own, regardless of seniority. Having accountability for your role means you are responsible for educating others in its importance, its outcomes and objectives, and how it will support the organization.

To ensure that this is clear, the accountability and ownership is documented for all to see and to buy in to. This can be provided via a delegation-of-authority model. In the absence of accountability, an 'empire builder' will always step in to take control. This is why it is important to spell out accountabilities and ensure they are adhered to. In many organizations, this is seen as part of an individual's job description; however, in the 10×Generation state, the elements of accountability are shared across the organization by linking role descriptions. Success measures become visible at every layer, and form part of the third principle: assessment (as discussed later).

Open communication

Each person employed has a voice, and visibility of the goings-on across the organization. Feedback is welcomed and scoped, to ensure risk is a consideration and that commentary is coming from areas of relevance, to prevent extraneous commentary bogging down productivity. As an example, if a proposal is put forward, each person will have a say as to how it would impact their area, whether the proposal is feasible, and the best way to achieve it based on their area of expertise. Ensuring that everyone has a clear mandate to keep technical or process debt to a minimum will drive the conversation towards doing what is in the organization's best interests.

This opening of communications means that communications will be heard and not easily dismissed, which will lead to 'intrinsic motivation'.[17] Everyone has a community to speak within. This basic understanding reduces contention, as individuals work out how to communicate across and within the operational, tactical and strategic layers.

Education and knowledge (the best leaders are great teachers)

In the 10×Generation state, a cornerstone is education and knowledge. Each individual is responsible for communicating the importance of their role and how it demonstrates value to the organization. Value creation has a direct link to the organization's strategic objectives and is mapped against them. To make this tenet possible, it is necessary to educate others so they understand each role within and across all layers. This includes what a role does, how it does it, and why certain decisions need to be made openly and not in isolation.

Like an organism, an organization is the sum of its parts, and each has to work symbiotically to continue to thrive. Educating each department will make the impacts of decisions clear and ensure that the best possible decision is made, given the information available.

Knowledge leads into an individual's curiosity. Enabling continuous learning means everyone in the organization has access to training and knowledge-sharing as needed. Models of success include peer programming, job shadowing, mentorships, buddy programmes and giving team members the time to undertake some form of sharing. This in turn ensures that, as decisions are made that reflect the continual understanding of the impacts of the decision on the organization, no one feels that they are in the dark on important decisions.

Once the first principle is embedded and seen in action, it is time to move on to the other principles, which can be addressed concurrently. Do not move too rapidly from this step. As it is the foundation of all the other principles, embedding this principle must be done with care and due diligence. Every team member must be taken along the journey together.

Second principle: Adaptation

For any organization to survive, it must adapt to changing conditions and embrace adaptation. From an evolutionary standpoint, adaptation arises from a need to change, and this applies to organizations becoming better suited to their environment. Unlike in the Agile/Scrum methodology, where adaptation is seen as an ability to improvise,[18] in the 10×Generation state, adaptation is the *culmination of curiosity, growth, alignment and value-driven thinking*, resulting in a prism of alignment (see Figure 12). This is not a replacement for other methodologies but a way of augmenting your organization to increase productivity and accelerate into the stratosphere.

Adaptation in the 10×Generation state is having the courage to make decisions that are aligned with the overall direction of the organization, regardless of management intervention. This can be achieved only in an organization that has a culture of psychological safety in place. Otherwise it could be career-limiting for individuals. It means having the confidence to lose people who no longer serve the direction of the organization, regardless of how long they have been there, and the courage to train and retain good talent. It is about a growth mindset that is firmly aligned with value-driven thinking.

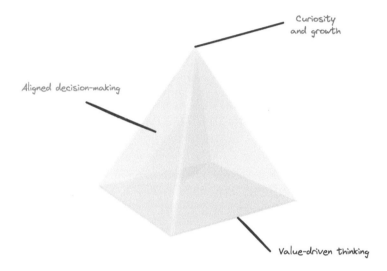

Figure 12 The prism of alignment

Curiosity and growth

Using the foundations of knowledge and education from the empowerment principle, we embrace the need for continued curiosity, which lends itself to a growth mindset. This mindset is vital in the 10×Generation state, as it enables an organization to continue to adapt to changing market pressures.

Curiosity at all layers broadens thinking and encourages constant improvement in ways of working. Stagnation is the embodiment of an organization that has lost its growth mindset. Complacency leads to digital transformations that ultimately do not work. In the 10×Generation state, curiosity and growth are fundamental in ensuring prosperity in the organization and for everyone it employs.

Aligned decision-making

Once the organization has embraced the tenet of accountability and ownership, aligned decision-making becomes easy. When everyone in the operational tier is aware of everyone else's objectives and how these align with the organization's needs and wants, alignment of decisions is an understood by-product.

Aligned decision-making ensures that every decision made that has a direct impact on the organization's growth and prosperity is in alignment with the organization's direction and individual measures of success. When a decision is made that connects horizontally and vertically across all layers, decision-making will always be aligned. Contention happens when alignment is not considered, and an individual's outcomes take precedence over those of the organization.

Value-driven thinking

In the 10×Generation state, value-driven thinking stems from the understanding that to stop the bloat in an organization, there always need to be at least three options presented for any people, process or practice decision being made. Each option needs to be value-driven in nature, and this in turn will enable the best decision to be made. Linking this thinking with aligned decision-making and all decisions will ultimately add value to the organization.

As discussed in the MIT Sloan article 'Creativity in decision-making with value-focused thinking',[19] 'value-focused thinking helps uncover hidden objectives' and leads to more productive information collection, which in turn provides more options for decision makers based on values derived during the problem-solving process. Being open to more than one option encourages 'outside-the-box' thinking and reinforces individual empowerment.

Value-driven thinking looks at the organization as a whole. By embedding this thinking, we start to see the skeleton of the 10×Generation state begin to take hold.

Third principle: Assessment

In the 10×Generation state, the focus is on assessing the right talent to be hired to do the job. We ensure that we hire the right people and then let them get on with it.[20] Measurements of success are driven by the organization's strategic intent. We allow the teams to measure the quality of their outputs, and we trust in those teams that we hired to deliver the product that the organization expects.

Measurement in the 10×Generation is based on intrinsically known organizational needs that align with overall objectives. The 10×Generation state removes the bottlenecks of decision-making and defines high-level targets that are to be achieved; this provides the individuals in each layer with the vision and allows them to come up with the way.

There are, however, a few key measurements that will bring the assessment principle to life. The three elements of the assessment principle are shown in Figure 13.

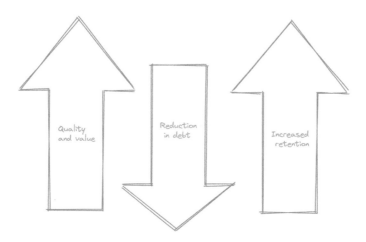

Figure 13 The three elements of the assessment principle

Quality and value

A by-product of empowerment is a continuous flow of outputs from all areas of the organization. Increased delivery is reframed and measured by quality and value creation. Gone is the need to measure each individual task that a team performs; instead, the focus is on the value that the team's outputs have created.

In the 10×Generation state, 'quality and value' means the increased efficiencies that an organization experiences when it is working in harmony across all layers. It is the by-product of an organization that has open communications and a clear vision of expectations that all have bought in to. Outcomes are seen in customer satisfaction, positive feedback and greater market share. If something needs to be measured, it is measured by use of product, customer engagement and increased profit margin.

Reduction in debt

The potential reduction of technical or process-related debt is a target embraced across all individuals in the organization. It is managed under an overarching and unifying process that ensures that addressing debt does not create additional risks. Dependencies are mapped and debt is actioned. Everyone, regardless of their role, will have the ability to impact the technical or process debt affecting the organization. The decisions that each individual makes, and the technology they use in their day-to-day activities, can impact debt.

The thing with debt is that eventually it needs to be repaid, and having this measured is the key to reduction. It is a way of thinking rather than a hard-and-fast measure that needs to be adhered to. This becomes a consideration, and requires that at least three options are presented with any technology or process decision that is needed. The three options provide the relevant information for assessment to be made to ensure that debt is always at the forefront of people's thinking in the 10×Generation state.

Increased retention

By empowering everyone across the organization, working towards agreed frameworks, embracing joint decision-making and promoting continuous improvement, we are creating a practice that all individuals aspire to. If we ensure that we have the courage to make the hard 'people' decisions, and are always considering the value we add to the organization, we will be able to measure staff retention. Improved retention is the 10×Generation way of showing that the right culture is being formed and is being bought into.

Fourth principle: Alignment

When researching for this publication, we met with multiple CEOs and asked the question of the importance of an organizational strategy. Whatever the size of the organization, whether it was a startup, a scaleup or larger, the same conclusion was provided: *create a strategy*. The strategy needs to provide the team with a picture of where the organization is placed in the market, and how customers and peers see it; it needs to be clear where the organization wants to play.

Without this alignment (as shown in Figure 14), the teams in the organization have no anchor point to hold on to, and this makes aligned decision-making impossible. Everyone needs an anchor point – a starting place, somewhere safe to return to – and this is what the strategy represents to an organization. The final factor in the creation of the strategy is understanding that as the organization evolves, so too will the strategy. It is a living document and needs to evolve with you.

Figure 14 The path to alignment nirvana

Organizational strategy

In the 10×Generation state, the creation of the strategy takes place in the strategic layer. However, the operational and tactical layers will also each need to have their own strategy, which will underpin the organization's overall strategy. The organizational strategy will need to outline the organization's growth aspirations, its goals, how it intends to meet these, and the overall organizational vision.

Departmental strategy

The departmental strategy will emulate the key areas of the organization's strategy and will fully align with its goals. Measures of success noted in the strategy will filter down to the individuals in the team. But remember that the way success is measured in the 10×Generation state differs from the use of standard business measurements. We allow teams to measure themselves and what they believe is important based on the needs of the strategy. Every department must have a strategy, and this must align with the organization's strategy.

This alignment is imperative across all areas of the business, but is most important in the engine room (operational layer), as this is the foundational layer for all organizations. If this is not aligned – you guessed it, yet another digital transformation or complete organizational restructure is on the cards!

Defined organizational design

Not Another Digital Transformation is not a guide to organizational design theory. The intent from the outset was to turn organizational design theory[21] on its head. To change the way all organizations operate. To empower everyone within to manage, deliver and own their destinies; to have visibility across, above and below; and to know that they have a voice.

The intent is to instil autonomy by providing guardrails to assist organizations during their transformation to this new state. There is no need for a multitude of management and hierarchy when an organization embraces the 10×Generation state. There is a need for clearly defined accountabilities that link to the strategy. This provides the anchor point and the vision for the future state.

What is organizational design theory?

Organizational design theory is a framework that outlines how a company should structure itself. There are many types of designs that will be nuanced by the type of goods and services the organization provides. For each framework, there will be pros and cons that may hinder or help the organization in growing and being successful.

An organization does not necessarily start with a structure in mind. If it is a startup, there may not be a structure, and this decision is made to ensure maximized outputs with minimal staffing. The intent of the startup is to create a product or service in the fastest time possible and seek further funding to grow the company. Everyone in the organization will be undertaking many roles, and no specific hierarchy is determined during the startup phase.

However, post-startup, when the organization has reached its first financial hurdles, the process of scaling begins. This is when organizational design theory will begin, whether deliberately or inadvertently. If the leadership understands traditional design theory, this is where hiring decisions will be made to flesh out the structure. If it does not, the organization will continue to grow organically. Neither practice is wrong: each has advantages and disadvantages.

From an organizational design theory perspective, there are two overarching structures that will resonate for many who read this publication. These structures describe the amount of management overhead needed to support the framework. Each will have pros and cons for the organization. The two theories we will discuss are the *tall* structure and the *flat* structure.

The tall structure works extremely well when there is a notion that employees need to be controlled. In this command-and-control model, there is a need for greater management overhead to control the actions and activities of employees.

The flat structure works in the opposite way. If the business wants its employees to have more autonomy and empowerment, a flat structure will be the preferred model. This structure has less management overhead.

With the tall structure, there are many levels, and there is a perceived view of greater autonomy as you move upwards through the structure, with greater options for career progression. In the flat structure, there is the perceived view that there are fewer opportunities for career advancement; however, the trade-off is greater autonomy at all levels.

Understanding exactly where your organization fits in these structures is important, to help you gauge what needs to be changed to improve overall efficiencies. If you are in a tall structure, the overhead of the management hierarchy may impact the speed to market of your goods and services. Alternatively, with the flat structure, there may be greater velocity if execution works well, but less career progression.

When considering the model being used in your organization, it is also important to understand the span of control, and the authority and accountability assigned to each person in the organization. In this theory, the span of control determines the number of employees a single manager can effectively manage without impacting the organization's overall efficiencies. Simply said, this means how many people one person can lead without losing control of their department. The authority that is given also needs to be considered, as too much authority at the wrong level can restrict a company's activities. Finally, accountability represents the checks and balances that are placed on the management positions.

Understanding the elements of organizational design theory is important, as it will give you the basis to understand the potential changes you will be faced with as you move towards the 10×Generation. All of these elements ensure effective business operations in the traditional office landscape; however, they are not necessarily the best way to structure your organization for the digital era.

Guidance for alignment

At the end of each script in Chapter 7, there will be actions and guidance to move to the 10×Generation state. As your organization will have varying challenges, these concepts are designed to help you improve your ways of working and to ensure you address the principles for the operational, tactical and strategic layers.

The success triad

As you progress through the 10×Generation principles, it is important to know what success will look like. As you embed the four principles, there are three overarching critical success factors that will ensure that your journey to the optimal state is achieved. We call this the *success triad* (see Figure 15).

Figure 15 The success triad

When instilling the four principles, it is important to confirm that the success triad is being met to ensure that you are on the right track to the 10×Generation state. The foundational measures of success relate to organizational alignment and are measured in the *org calibration* metrics.

Org calibration

This measure will ensure that every single person understands, and is on board with, the strategic direction of the organization, and what they and their team are doing to achieve this. This measure looks at each tier – operational, tactical and strategic – and the goals put in place that align with the organization's blueprint.

The individual departments put together departmental goals or OKRs (objectives and key results) that align with the strategy and are measured on the basis of agreed outcomes. The objectives are rated across the department for alignment, which then flows across to all other departments. The purpose is to seek multilateral calibration across the entire organization.

To rate each OKR, determine whether it addresses these questions:

- Does it meet the organization's growth aspirations?
- Does it align with the organization's values?
- Does it enable others to achieve their goals as well as those of the individual, team or department?

If each question is acknowledged with a resounding 'yes', the OKR rates as 3/3. If it does not, it rates lower. The intent is to have all OKRs as 3/3.

The OKRs are reviewed and debated in an *open forum* across the business to ensure that there is alignment. This is what differentiates the 10×Generation process from other approaches.

Every individual must have sight of all objectives across the business, as they may be impacted by them. Ownership and visibility for all is necessary for org calibration to be successful.

Waste elimination

There are many ways of reducing waste in your organization, and the Lean concepts are discussed in Chapter 5 (see box on 'What is waste?'). We have all seen the power of continuous improvement and the Six Sigma movement, but there is so much more to waste elimination than just following the Lean concepts.

In the 10×Generation state, each team member in each department in each tier has clear visibility of the ways of working, and how they interface with all other teams and departments. The hard part is ensuring that the right measures are in place to ensure that this visibility enables the measures to make a marked difference to the organization's overall velocity and productivity.

Waste means different things to each department – it could be people, process, technology, cost and so on – but needs to be looked at from all views in the department. For our purposes, we will focus on five of the areas of waste: waiting, overproduction, overprocessing, defects and skills.

- **Waiting** This is the absence of, or the delay in, receiving the information and data needed to make relevant and timely decisions. It represents blockers, where silos do not communicate across the organization, and information and decisions are missed or lost, or time to respond is elongated, impacting efficiencies
- **Overproduction** This is where there are too many silos, and a lack of visibility and successful communication across them, inevitably leading to effort being duplicated
- **Overprocessing** This is where there is a lack of communication with decision makers. Overprocessing takes place when the wrong people make decisions for the organization, and produce products or services that are not necessarily needed or wanted
- **Defects** This is a direct result of silos not communicating across the organization. It is a result of overproduction, and means that rework is required to re-align the provided products and services to the overall business strategy

- **Skills** This is a key area of focus for this publication. Because the leadership does not understand or recognize the organization's talent pool, it sees a need to fill positions with additional headcount. When a leader is not recognized, a new middle manager is hired. This blinkered approach to skills is one of the main causes of organizational bloat.

In each department, you will look at the waste in all three tiers and determine what can be eliminated. Ensure that this elimination waste feeds into org calibration.

Sufficiency realization

In the 10×Generation state, each tier, and each department in it, becomes self-sufficient. Everything can be achieved without noise and drama. OKRs are clear; alignment is achieved. However, each department must be able to run independently when needed, and must understand its interdependencies with other departments and how to make these work seamlessly.

Think of a micro-department, analogous to a microservice, that can operate on its own but also can operate as part of the whole. To achieve this, there is an embedding of support and departmental roles, which are represented as part of each 'micro-department'.

The operational tier includes key personnel who represent functions such as HR, recruitment, finance and marketing. These have reporting lines into the leadership of the operational tier and visibility of the tactical and strategic department leadership. Success is measured by the upskilling and embedding of support functions in the tiers and in the departments, further building out the concept of cross-functional teams:

- Roles and responsibilities are mapped to individuals who will undertake the supporting functions in the department
- Training plans to upskill are implemented and secondments are included.

When designing your organization, you want to think that if you were to sell the business, every micro-department could be sold independently without impacting the other departments.

By ensuring that there is a focus on the success triad as the four principles are embedded, you will provide a firm foundation for the 10×Generation state. A caveat, however, is that a transformation of this type is daunting. It can be scary for an organization that is set in its ways, but the alternative of undertaking yet another digital transformation in an effort to improve efficiencies and improve market share is just as harrowing. The actions to embed the principles in this publication are not exhaustive, and there are more ideas that can be implemented, but these will get you well on the path to the 10×Generation state.

The key point, however, is this: focus on embedding all four principles across all three tiers, otherwise this will not work. You cannot have visibility only in the engine room and expect change.

7 The scripts

To bring *Not Another Digital Transformation* to life, we have provided scripts for three acts of a play. Each script is intended to give examples of conversations that may have happened in real-life situations. They target the various personas in an organization, and provide options on how to deal with each scenario being experienced. These actions will bring you closer to the 10×Generation state and enable you to guide your organization in achieving this.

By shifting the dial towards this state, you will in turn gain maximum velocity along the way. As there are multiple ways to approach any given scenario, the authors have provided preferences to advise you. Each step can and should be measured as you make your way to the 10×Generation state. The scripts will enable you to start thinking, planning and preparing for the next step in your 10×Generation journey. They will give insight and prepare you for the challenges ahead.

Act 1: The tragedy of a digital transformation

In Act 1 we will focus on issues that are faced when working in the operational layer of an organization (see Figure 16). This is where the foundation of the product and technology departments will reside. Regardless of the structure, there will always be a product and technology layer, although it may be represented differently between organizations.

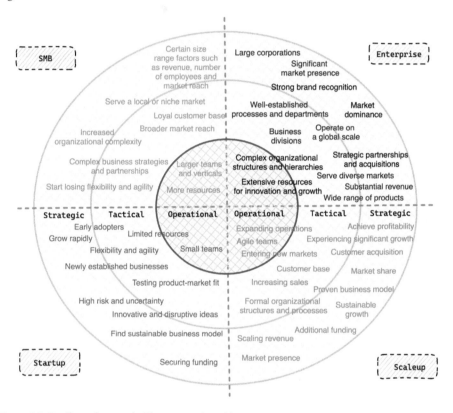

Figure 16 Radius of growth: The operational layer

Product and technology is often considered the engine room, as it supports all other business functions. However, the key thing to recognize is that whatever the size of the organization, the engine room needs to be supported and needs to continually evolve. Without evolution, the technology will age and slow, and this will have a direct impact on every other layer and ultimately impact the organization's growth strategy. Just keeping the lights on is not enough, and many organizations eventually face the uncomfortable truth that they will need to invest significantly to keep the business functioning.

It is at this moment that the inevitable digital transformation project will be initiated. Most projects of this kind are the by-product of a lack of planning and strategic vision across the organization, and not the fault of the product and technology department alone. For many in product and technology, the organization structure is misaligned, which includes reporting lines, and this will have direct repercussions. When technology is seen only as a cost centre and not a value-add, any funding requests are seen as a hindrance to the bottom line, regardless of the potential benefits of the request.

Unfortunately, when an organization focuses solely on the operational view, a digital transformation is destined to fail, as technology will be the main consideration. Instead of thinking about how the three layers in the organization should work together and be aligned, the plan of attack will be to revolutionize the technology. With a revolutionary lens focusing on operations as the only viable option, it is no wonder that so many digital transformations fail.

Given that the operational view has its own operational, tactical and strategic views, it is important that each of these layers is aligned with the broader business vision, and has the strategy to continuously evolve and maintain any technical debt accumulated on its journey to scale.

Disclaimer: All characters appearing in this work are fictitious. Any resemblance to real persons, living or dead, is purely coincidental.

Setting the operational scene

In this first act, we are introduced to the characters in our organizations. Each organizational type is represented – startup or scaleup, SMB and enterprise – although when reading it will become apparent that most scenarios will fit any size of organization. Each character represents a role that is instrumental in the functioning of the operational layer and shows how misalignment, silos and lack of vision can impact the characters.

Each scene gives the reader a version of a conversation that may take place in a business. No matter what role you may play or the size of your organization, you will be provided with strategies to overcome the difficulties our characters find themselves in. At the start of each script, hashtags are used to help define the type of organization and layer that it would potentially play out in.

Startup or scaleup

A startup or scaleup organization will need to prove itself as an organizational contender. About 90% of startups fail, and 10% fail within the first year.[22] If it makes it past this first hurdle and grows into the scaleup phase, ensuring the foundation for the business is well thought out will be imperative to ongoing success.

The following scenarios are felt in many of these organization types, and addressing them immediately will go a long way towards ensuring greater sustainability.

Act 1, Scene 1: When bloat leads to silos

#Startup #Scaleup #SMB #Enterprise

#Operational #Tactical

With additional growth, we start to see more layers. This can be of benefit in some scenarios, but in this scene we will show what happens when it is ill-considered. Senior leadership is seeing more requests for headcount than it had originally budgeted for. Instead of work being balanced across team members and the right work being in the right places, there are single points of failure, with team members holding all knowledge and building empires. Silos are being created, and there is a misalignment across the business as to what is actually needed, as individuals have lost focus on what is important.

We find ourselves in the chief information officer's (CIO's) office, where a heated discussion is well underway.

Lights come up on our main protagonist, the IT operations engineer (Joey), in deep discussion with the CIO (Ajay), advising him of the need for more staff to support his growing team of support engineers.

Narrator	When this startup began its life, there were a handful of team members with the same vision: to grow their application into a product that everyone needs. They employed some young guns to propel the development further and faster, but now, as the startup grows, they are seeing individuals burning out from the pressure of growth. However, with this growth there is a reluctance to empower others.
CIO (Ajay)	Joey, I understand that you need more operations engineers, but I'm concerned about the costs. What other options do you have?
IT ops engineer (Joey)	*(Heated)* I have no other options! I'm currently managing everything from reliability to deployments to quality testing. I need more people, otherwise my team and I will burn out! We can't possibly keep up the velocity we're working at now without some casualties!
CIO (Ajay)	Calm down, Joey. The remit of your role is reliability, so why are you involved in deployments and quality testing?
IT ops engineer (Joey)	*(Heated)* Oh, come on, Ajay! There isn't anyone stepping up to the quality side of things, and if you think I'm going to let the developers deploy into my systems, then you have another think coming. My team have to support this app, and we need to control what goes into it. If you want 'follow the sun' support, then I need more people! If you want better quality, I need more people! It's simple maths.

CIO (Ajay)	I know you've been with us since the start, Joey, and I appreciate the work you and your team do.
	I think you've taken a lot of additional work on which doesn't really sit under the remit of your and your team's role. I appreciate that you've stepped in to help this business grow, but there must be a smarter way of doing this rather than throwing additional headcount at it.
IT ops engineer (Joey)	I think I should own all deployments for the application, and be in charge of quality testing as well. If I don't have a final say as to what goes into the application, then I can't be held accountable for its reliability.
	I do a lot of work here, Ajay, and without me this company would be in a lot of trouble.
	I'm asking for more headcount so that I can be certain that we have a reliable system. I need to own these other areas for quality's sake!
CIO (Ajay)	Joey, I hear you, but you need to stay within the remit of your role. I need you to hand over the deployment and quality tasks to the teams who are responsible for them. It isn't up to you alone, as to what can or cannot be deployed.
Narrator	Ajay knows that the application needs to be supported, but does not have enough visibility into what is really needed to support it. The rapid growth of the business from startup to scaleup created gaps that needed to be filled. Now, however, Joey has started to build an empire, which he is reluctant to let go of, even if it is better for the business. As more people are hired, the cost begins to escalate under the guise of ensured supportability.

Six months later.

Narrator	The organization continues on its rapid growth trajectory, and the CIO has not revisited the operations team since the original conversation. Our engineer does not focus on transferring knowledge to others. He continues to remain the single point of failure for the business. Nothing has changed, with his empire well entrenched in the business, causing an underlying dependency on him and a risk to the organization.

Stage lights dim and we fade to black.

10×Generation

Single points of failure in the scaleup or SMB space are a common by-product of rapid growth from a startup business. People who start in the early days of a startup step into areas that they are not necessarily proficient in. In the absence of an owner, the role will be filled by other people from within the organization. In a startup, this is applauded – but as the business grows, there is a need to review those who are in roles that may not serve the organization's best interests. If a role grows well outside of its areas of accountability, an empire builder can become just as destructive as bloating an organization.

Embedding the 10×Generation principles will make achieving efficiencies a reality. The following list provides further details on what is possible:

- For the organization to scale efficiently, all team members need to be empowered and provided with visibility across it. This is achieved by having clearly defined roles and responsibilities
- This visibility of what the individual is accountable for, and what the organization expects from them, must be known and accessible to all in the team, tier and organization
- When each team member is aware of overall expectations, an empire builder is unable to get a foothold in the organization. The expectations of each individual are defined when they join the organization and are reviewed periodically to ensure that they meet ongoing business expectations
- Focusing on implementing the first principle of empowerment, and embedding education and knowledge transfer, will address the skills gap that will be a side-effect of an empire builder working in the organization.

The solution lies in the empowerment of all for the betterment of the business, and putting ego to one side. In the 10×Generation state, empire building has no place and needs to be curbed in its infancy. Clarity comes from a transparent culture and clearly defined organizational design.

The solution to empire building is creating an environment where teams work hand in hand, in constant communication with consistent, respectful feedback. If you are already battling silos, embracing a cross-functional teams structure will help in breaking this down. You can find more on this in Act 2, Scene 12: 'Resistance to cross-functional teams – The team of teams revolution'.

If you have successfully addressed overblown staffing of the organization, this will have a positive effect from an EBITDA* perspective and also on morale. Destructive behaviours become a thing of the past.[23]

The next area to be addressed is the structure of the teams. To maintain harmony, there is a need to focus on removing communication barriers. Let's see what happens when barriers are created in our next scene.

---

* EBITDA stands for earnings before interest, taxes, depreciation and amortization. EBITDA measures the company's overall financial performance.

Act 1, Scene 2: Product and technology separation anxiety

#Startup #Scaleup #SMB

#Operational #Tactical

In any organization, the arrival or departure of a CIO, chief technology officer (CTO) or chief product officer (CPO) can send other C-level executives (or their equivalent) into a tailspin. There is confusion surrounding the cyclical debate over whether product and technology should remain under one department or be split into separate departments.

This decision will have direct implications across the entire organization, and if the wrong choice is made, it will impact the organization's ability to increase velocity. Without alignment across product and technology, there will be a negative impact on velocity of delivery.

We find ourselves in the company boardroom as the lights come up on stage.

The stage is set with the arrival of a new CIO, Ajay, who has not been part of the digital transformation that is still fresh among everyone in the product and technology space. The head of product (Roberto) and acting CTO (Andrea) are waiting eagerly to see what the new boss will bring to their roles and the organization.

Narrator	Many moons ago, there was a CTO and a CPO who wanted to achieve increased agility and increased productivity. They convinced the CEO that the organization needed better alignment between product and technology, and combined these departments into one as part of a bigger reorganization. Enter Ajay, our new CIO with a Harvard degree. A meeting is called in Ajay's office to discuss the plans for the next financial year, with Ken (CEO), Ajay (CIO), Lakshmi (chief financial officer – CFO) and Andrea (acting CTO, previously head of technology).
CEO (Ken)	Ajay, our product has not necessarily been the best in the market, and we're struggling with even delivering parity. Other organizations seem to be releasing new features every month and stealing our share of the marketplace.
CIO (Ajay)	I've seen this many times in my past life, Ken. The challenge you're facing is that we need to bring a product management mindset shift into this business.
CFO (Lakshmi)	I heard that from our previous CPO, and I'm not sure what he meant. We spent a few million dollars on a digital transformation last year, and we were promised that the product and technology teams would be more agile, another word that I don't seem to understand! We were supposed to be faster, but I haven't seen it.

CIO (Ajay)	We need to shift the discussion from 'technology initiatives' and 'project managers' to 'customer experience'. It means evaluating my team's performance on business outcomes, not on whether we deliver a solution on time or on budget.
Acting CTO (Andrea)	And what does that mean?
CIO (Ajay)	It means reorganizing the product and technology teams so they can get closer to our customer. Make each department accountable for their own deliverables instead of hiding behind each other. Two separate departments, each held responsible.
CEO (Ken)	Ajay, I would love to have that – it aligns with our core values. Can you please discuss with Lakshmi on the budget implications and come back to me on how we would achieve this?
Acting CTO (Andrea)	(Playing on Andrea's phone) Song 1. Not Again by Staind.[24] Track 1/10

Six weeks after the meeting

Narrator	Ajay has now hired a new CTO (Jane), and the acting CTO (Andrea) has been moved back into her regular day job. A new CPO, Alec, has also been hired. The new hires report into Ajay and have added many more roles since their arrival. Our CFO (Lakshmi) is not very happy with the increasing costs in the CIO office, but this is how most modern organizations achieve scale and increase agility, isn't it? The business is about to hit the end of the financial year, and there are no metrics that show any difference in how the company has performed, including speed to market or better product for the customers. How will Ajay provide Ken with the outcomes he had promised?

10×Generation

This is a common scenario in most organizations, where they are in an infinite loop of moving product and technology under the same roof, only to then separate them to improve scale.

The biggest challenge the product and technology departments face are the lines of accountability for 'technology versus product'. The solution sits in between what a startup would do and what a seasoned CIO would do in terms of scaling:

- Bring in a blended team structure where the product and technology leaderships report into the same C-level leader

- Remove translation and communication barriers, helping product managers, product owners, programme managers and business analysts to avoid having to go round in circles on what's needed. Bring the product and technology teams together, so they're not just sitting next to each other but also reporting into the same senior leadership with the same goals

- Have everyone in product and technology understand the full lifecycle from the product's inception through to the product in the customer's hand, and the measures of success after launch (with business and technology metrics treated as equally important)

- The product and technology group treats both internal and external customers with the same care and love that they need

- Leadership ensures there are no silos; product and technology leaders are influencing rather than owning teams.

Gartner says: 'Digital business is treated as a team sport by CEOs and no longer the sole domain of the IT department'.[25] The benefits are clear when a blended structure is implemented (Figure 17).

Figure 17 When the blended structure is implemented, the benefits are clear

In order for this team sport to be truly successful, there needs to be a focus on winning the season, not just winning the game. To win the season, a team needs a clearly defined strategy. Let's see what happens if it doesn't have one.

Act 1, Scene 3: Don't worry, advisers will fix it!

#Startup #Scaleup #SMB #Enterprise #LargeEnterprise

#Operational #Tactical #Strategic

In its optimal state, an organization has clearly defined outcomes that it needs to achieve in the long term. In the 10×Generation state, each tier has its own strategy that links back to the organization's strategic intent. Each department is clear on what the other departments need, and this provides clarity to all on how the outcomes will be achieved.

Unfortunately, when an organization is in its startup phase, the need for a strategy is not seen as important. The only needs that are seriously considered are to raise capital, build market share, deliver a product that is wanted and keep growing. This works well if you're a startup, but becomes problematic as the business starts to scale.

For many startups, there comes a time when its leaders realize they believe they do not have the relevant skills needed to continue to grow, and the questions are asked: 'If our people don't have the skills needed, should we bring in advisers to help? Will they resolve the talent shortfall and provide guidance to resolve the tactical problems we're facing? Should we develop our strategy first?'

In the absence of a strategy or at least some form of strategic intent, we will see how the conversation evolves and the outcomes that are achieved.

The CTO of the organization, Jane, sits at her desk, looking frustrated. She picks up her laptop and opens a Zoom call with the head of technology, Andrea. A calendar on the wall behind her shows the current month and year.

CTO (Jane)	*(Looking into her laptop)* Hi, Andrea. I think I've decided that we need to bring in some consultants, as the DevOps teams are struggling to hire new people. We don't have a strategy in place, and I need to start sharing our cloud cost breakdown with our CFO.
Head of technology (Andrea)	There is no way to do this unless we have tagged all our resources and have a tagging strategy in place.
Narrator	Jane looks frustrated and taps her pen on the desk. A stack of papers and a computer are on the desk in front of her. She knows that a tagging strategy requires significant work, as keywords are assigned to all assets and this takes time to implement – valuable time that they do not have.
CTO (Jane)	I know, I know. But we're in a bind here and we need some outside help. Can you put together a plan for how we can use consultants effectively without a formal strategy in place?

Andrea thinks for a moment, then nods. A filing cabinet and a plant are in the corner of the office.

Head of technology (Andrea)	Sure, I can put together a plan. But I strongly recommend that we develop a strategy before bringing in consultants. Or we at least think about where we want to be heading as an organization. This will make their work more effective and save us time and money in the long run. If we don't have a view, how will we know if they've delivered what we want?

Cut to present day: Checkpoint – 1 month before consultants finish up.

CTO (Jane)	That was a good meeting. I liked that they prepared a state of DevOps report for us.
Head of technology (Andrea)	They didn't tell us anything that our engineers haven't already told us.
CTO (Jane)	You don't have to be so negative, Andrea. I think the report they produced was really useful.
Head of technology (Andrea)	I just wish they'd had more of a view of our needs, so they wouldn't have duplicated what we already had. I do have to concede that their report is well polished, but we already know this stuff.
Narrator	Even though the consultancy had suggested some really good ideas, it ended up working on a tagging strategy, which was a one-time activity.
	Six months later, the consultants are gone and the tagging strategy hasn't been embedded in the processes and practices. The cost breakdown reports have become stale, and no one knows how to fix them, as they were never transitioned. Andrea has resigned as the head of technology, and her replacement, Mike, says he has inherited rubbish.

10×Generation

Without a clearly defined strategy and outcomes to deliver value, we find an organization that has paid consulting fees for outcomes that had already been defined. We have unsupportable reporting that was never embedded and ways of working that didn't stick.

When consultants are engaged, clearly knowing what you need to be delivered ensures that you create a value proposition that is easily quantifiable. When consultants are engaged at the expense of team members and the teams are not engaged in the process, the result is employee dissatisfaction and potential retention issues.

In the 10×Generation state, all employees are empowered within their sphere of influence. They are provided with the same information, and everyone has a voice. If silos are broken down above and below, plans can be aligned and immediately provide value to the organization. Then, if consulting experience is needed, this decision is made with a clear view of expectations from within the teams.

When there are no clearly aligned strategies, we can see actions taking place that have the potential to derail team outputs. In the next scene, we see what happens when teams are not empowered and silos are proposed in an effort to speed up delivery.

Act 1, Scene 4: To ringfence or not to ringfence?

#Startup #Scaleup #SMB #Enterprise #LargeEnterprise

#Operational #Tactical #Strategic

In a 10×Generation state, there are very few, if any, isolated teams working on individual projects. In its simplest form, the 10×Generation state is one of complete collaboration across the entire organization, with everyone understanding the outcome that needs to be achieved, and everyone working cohesively towards it.

When we separate the teams and create pockets, we create barriers that impact communications and embed a culture of 'us versus them'. No single project is more important than the entire organization's strategy unless the entire organization is allowed to express views on the decision and has an input into it. Here we find product and technology fighting a losing battle.

The scene is a virtual conference call, where the heads of product and technology are discussing the plan to resource the team.

Narrator	Product and technology has been tasked by the business executive with the creation of a separate, isolated team. The purpose of the request is to allow the team to focus on specific goals and objectives without external distractions or interference. Ultimately the executive wants to increase delivery, and believes that if teams are isolated and focusing on what is deemed important, the velocity on the meaningful work will improve.
Head of product (Roberto)	Thanks for joining the call, Mike. As you know, we need to ringfence a team.
Head of technology (Mike)	Sorry, before we start: can you explain exactly what 'ringfencing' means?

Head of product (Roberto)	By ringfencing, I mean we need to ensure that the new team will have dedicated resources and a dedicated operating model. We don't want the team distracted by outside influences. It needs to be separate in order to succeed.
Head of technology (Mike)	Got it. And what about collaboration with other teams?
Head of product (Roberto)	During the ringfencing period, the new team will be expected to work independently and not seek assistance or input from other teams, unless absolutely necessary. This is a temporary arrangement, and once the ringfencing period is over, the team will be expected to reintegrate and collaborate with other teams as per our ways of working.
Head of technology (Mike)	As you would have experienced yourself, we have a services catalogue and most teams own areas of technology. It's naïve to think a new project won't touch any other area in our technical stack. And have you thought about all the ancillary roles? Like DevOps engineers, solution architects, etc.? Are we ringfencing them as well?
Narrator	The meeting ends with the management principle of 'Agree to disagree but commit'.[26] Mike agrees to stand up a new team by pulling people from their existing teams, causing a priority challenge.

10×Generation

In the operational view, executives who are not from a technology background need significant education on the way effective technology teams work. No technology team works in an isolated manner.

When this is attempted, it increases the risk of errors in the end product, duplication of effort, and technical debt.

This leads to higher costs (both tangible and intangible), longer project timelines and eventually having to revisit areas of code that were developed in isolation. The education piece is a key outcome of the 10×Generation state, and forms part of the journey to increased velocity and decreased bloat.

Isolating teams to improve efficiencies is old-school thinking. Gone are the days when throwing resources at a problem would solve it. Ensuring that teams and processes are aligned, and that collaboration takes place ubiquitously, will ensure that important work is prioritized and delivered. If there are market changes and the organization needs to adapt rapidly, this can be achieved only with collaboration and joint decision-making. Unilateral decisions will always create silos and misalignment. If one person or department believes that their needs outweigh those of all other people and departments, this is when efficiencies are lost.

Although this is not an exhaustive set of scenarios, they are the key scenarios that can derail the startup or scaleup and lead to a failure to thrive.

Small-to-medium business

In the SMB organization, the scenarios vary in their complexity. An SMB generally has far more employees than a startup or scaleup, and will have a more hierarchical structure. It is in the SMB organization that we will see a tall structure being implemented as the foundation. From the early days of rapid delivery and a struggle to survive, the SMB will be challenged by different scenarios that will have the same effect of struggling to thrive.

In the 10×Generation state, every role has a voice, and every outcome demonstrated can be presented by anyone in the organization. The command-and-control model is replaced by empowerment, accountability and responsibility. The sense of ownership increases, as do velocity of delivery and employee satisfaction.

Here we see in our first scene the impact that command-and-control has on the organization.

Act 1, Scene 5: New leader, more processes, less delivery!

#SMB #Enterprise #LargeEnterprise

#Operational #Tactical

The organization decides it's time to appoint a new leader to bring rigour and process to the business. It recruits an operations manager (Bill), who is reporting into the CTO (Jane) and is key to implementing new processes.

In this script, various IT terms will be mentioned including *ITIL*, which is an IT framework, and *change advisory board* (CAB), used to track IT changes.

With this addition, we see more layers being added to an already resource-heavy organization with a misaligned structure and silos impacting delivery targets. This means having more managers, more administration and more processes – which, if not fully integrated, will cause an increase in barriers, impacting the organization's ability to deliver greater value to its customers.

> *Our scene opens in the main tea room, where the CTO (Jane) is announcing the need for greater rigour in the operations and saying that change is necessary to improve delivery across the team.*

Narrator	When our organization began its life, there were basic processes in place enabling the technology team to deliver on the original business vision. As the organization has grown, there has been little focus on processes, with a stronger focus on more technology to support the growing changes in the product roadmap.
	As the product evolved, so did the technology footprint; however, with this growth came additional cost. To support the technology landscape, additional headcount was needed. In order to curb the bloat of additional headcount, the CTO brings in another leader to fix the process problems. The thinking is that more processes will streamline the technology output, and more layers will ensure greater governance.
CTO (Jane)	*(Addressing the product and technology organization)* Good morning, team. I hope you had a great weekend and are ready for another big week. I wanted to gather you here to introduce the newest member of the leadership team.

Faint mumblings are heard from the product and technology team.

CTO (Jane)	After great discussion with our CEO, I have determined that in order to move our business forward we need to focus on our processes. Our velocity has slowed down considerably and we need to be better. We need to be able to support the growth aspirations of this business, and we cannot do this with our current ways of working. Therefore it gives me great pleasure to introduce Bill, our new operations manager, who will report directly into me.
P&T team	*(Staff sentiment) Here we go, more processes bogging down our ability to deliver. Why does management do this? Keep bringing in more leaders instead of asking us what we need?*
Operations manager (Bill)	Hello everyone, I'm Bill, and it's a pleasure to be joining the team. As Jane has mentioned, there is change coming. I am a firm believer in transparency, so I want to be clear. My job is to improve the way we do things around here. I have clear objectives to meet and I will be pushing to meet them. I have a proven track record in other businesses doing just that. We need to work together, but make no mistake, things here will change. The first thing I will be looking at are the processes we have in place. I will be implementing ITIL first up, and if you don't know what a change advisory board is, you soon will!
CTO (Jane)	Fantastic! So good to have you on board. Well, that's all for now. Let's get on with it.

| Narrator | Without any consultation, the product and technology team are informed of impending changes to their ways of working. When the organization was a startup, there were open channels of communication. Everyone was part of something new and they were involved in decisions, process improvements, and hiring and firing of team members. Now as the organization has grown, decisions are made without consultation, and this is creating disharmony across all teams. |

Dagmar (principal engineer) and Roberto are angry at the situation and speak conspiratorially to each other.

Principal engineer (Dagmar)	This is rubbish! How would Jane know what processes we use? She hasn't spent any time talking to us – she just buries her head in budget reports. If she had any idea, she would have asked us what we think we need. I don't understand the need to bog us down with more processes. How will a change advisory board work when we use continuous integration and continuous development? This operations manager, what was his name – Bill? We need to discuss the processes we follow and look at how we can implement ITIL principles that can enhance our automation. There has to be a way to bridge the gap between automation and additional frameworks.
Head of product (Roberto)	I agree. There was a time when we could have open and honest conversations, but it feels like our voice is no longer heard. There are so many management layers, it's hard to keep track. We have less visibility and less autonomy.
Narrator	With increased management layers, lack of visibility and little consultation, the organization starts to experience significant impacts on retention. In a climate where good technology resource is hard to come by, and with resignations on the increase, the organization is in trouble. Something needs to be done to curb the haemorrhaging that it's experiencing.

Stage lights dim and we fade to black.

10×Generation

As an organization grows from startup to a larger organization, the old way of thinking would be to add management layers to control the team members. Generally this is done without consultation, creates immediate barriers to change and creates silos in the organization. Silos and lack of visibility increase bottlenecks, which impact the velocity of the product and technology teams.

Many people who choose to work in startups do so because they want greater visibility and control over their destinies. In the startup, there is less bureaucracy to contend with, and if a process change is needed, it is done across all areas of the product and technology space. Everyone has a say, and agreement is met in an open and transparent way.

The solution in this instance is about removing barriers to success, not about bringing in additional layers of bureaucracy:

- Reduce layers of management and empower team members. The simple act of active listening goes a long way in empowering teams
- Review leadership roles to see what value they add and how they create more leaders, not more managers
- Review processes and technology on a regular basis, but ensure that this is done in an open forum. Your team knows what needs to change and what is needed to improve; simply asking it goes a long way in building trust and moving the business forward
- The command-and-control model represents old thinking when it comes to managing the throughput of team members. Removing barriers of communication and removing silos enables team members to work together, cohesively.

When we embed the 10×Generation's first principle, empowerment, we see barriers removed and communication pathways opened. This then enables individuals to have a say and to see where others are adding value. In many SMBs there will be employees who have been with the organization since the beginning and may be seen as senior to others. Tenure should not guarantee promotion; if it does, this can have significant consequences for the harmony of your teams. This is often known as the Peter Principle[27] and can be seen when a startup rapidly grows into a scaleup. Individuals may suffer from unconscious incompetence, which can increase the bureaucracy experienced in an organization. The more uncomfortable an individual feels, the more checks and balances are wrapped around a process, which in turn create greater bureaucracy. We suggest removing management layers to streamline communications.

When an organization suffers from having too many management layers, excuses to cover for failed delivery outcomes can cause friction points. When regulatory bodies are involved, there can be instances where one team attempts to stall other teams by using regulations and penalties as a mechanism of control.

Act 1, Scene 6: Regulating the imaginary – a journey of fictional regulations

#SMB #Enterprise #LargeEnterprise

#Operational #Tactical #Strategic

This is a common scenario where regulatory requirements are entirely concocted to support another team's agenda. Whether you are a policy enthusiast, a fan of satire or simply curious about the boundaries of regulatory fiction, this is one of the most common situations we have all seen and can place ourselves in.

Our scene opens in a big meeting room known as the 'Regulators' Den'. A team of project managers and engineers are gathered around a table discussing a new software development project. The senior project manager (PM), Jackson, is standing up and holding a piece of paper.

Senior PM (Jackson)	All right, everyone, I need your attention. We've just received word from Compliance that we need to implement Regulation XYZ for this project.
Technology leader (Hong)	What is this regulation?
Senior PM (Jackson)	Well, according to Compliance, it's a requirement that we have a change advisory board in place for every change that we make to the software. This is so all changes can be tracked.
Principal engineer (Dagmar)	A change advisory board? That sounds like a lot of unnecessary bureaucracy.
Senior PM (Jackson)	I know it sounds like a hassle, but it's a regulation that we have to follow.
Principal engineer (Dagmar)	Jackson, did someone actually tell you that we need a change board? Or is that just their interpretation of what the regulation says?
Head of architecture (Cillian)	*(Sceptically)* I don't think that's what the regulation says. Sometimes people confuse their own implementation of a regulation with what is actually required. We should go to the source and see what it actually says.
Senior PM (Jackson)	*(Defensively)* But we have to follow what Compliance says, right?
Principal engineer (Dagmar)	Exactly. Most compliance measures exist for good reasons – it's just the current implementation that makes them pointless and silly.

Technology leader (Hong)	*(Nodding)* And in our case, an automated verification of code review would satisfy the requirement far more effectively.
Narrator	Jackson looks uncertain, but the team is determined.
Head of architecture (Cillian)	Let's do this the right way and make sure we're not just ticking boxes.

10×Generation

It is wise to avoid simply reading a manual and completing an ineffective box-ticking process to support a regulatory requirement that may or may not be mandated by the regulation. When people rigidly adhere to the requirements of a regulation, they may fail to account for the context of the situation. This can lead to a direction where the regulation is applied in a way that does not make sense or is not effective.

One should make an effort to examine the source documentation to understand the regulatory framework and context of the requirement. It may then be appropriate to use automation to ensure that the regulation's intent is fully realized.

It is worth noting that regulations exist for valid reasons, but implementations, which may involve superficial paperwork and unproductive processes, often detract from their intended impact. Also, failing to adhere to the actual intent of regulations can result in compliance issues, legal problems and potential reputational damage. Simply meeting the prescribed checklist requirements without understanding the underlying purpose of the regulation can lead to suboptimal outcomes, thereby defeating the entire purpose of the regulation.

It is, therefore, crucial to approach regulatory compliance with a comprehensive understanding of the intent behind it. This will enable the organization to devise effective strategies that prioritize the intended outcomes of the regulations, rather than focusing solely on meeting the regulatory requirements.

Furthermore, automation can be an essential tool for achieving effective regulatory compliance. By automating compliance processes, an organization can streamline compliance procedures, reduce errors and increase efficiency. Additionally, automation can provide greater accuracy and consistency in the implementation of regulatory requirements, thus reducing the risk of non-compliance.

When agreement is sought regarding regulatory functions, we can see greater outcomes achieved. It is important to seek understanding, as this ensures that the decisions made can be adhered to. When decisions are made without an understanding of what is possible, we see issues of under-delivery.

Act 1, Scene 7: Rock-solid priorities: the cost of neglecting big rocks

#Scaleup #SMB #Enterprise #LargeEnterprise

#Operational #Tactical

In many organizations we see leaders continually faced with difficult decisions, whether these be about prioritization, technology or people management. The big rocks,[28] or the key things that must be achieved in an organization, must be aligned across all departments. Without alignment of key initiatives, we find leaders being forced to agree to untenable requests from leaders higher up in the hierarchy. In this scenario, we find a technology leader forced to accede to the request from a senior executive, knowing that the request will create significant work in the long term.

A lack of understanding of what it takes to deliver technical solutions from senior leaders puts IT professionals into situations that will always disappoint stakeholders, strain team well-being, impact credibility in levels of management and create technical debt.

There is no correct answer in this scenario for the technology leader. If they agree to what the executive asks for, there can only be one of two outcomes:

- Delivery is met by burning out the team – impacting retention, creating disharmony and generating technical debt
- The senior executive is disappointed, and the technical leader may find themselves out of a job.

Lights come up on a sparsely furnished office. The technology leader is sitting at his desk, staring at a request from upper management. The request is unrealistic and would be near-impossible to complete within the given timeframes without generating significant technical debt and burning out key team members.

Technology leader (Hong)	*(Sighs and thinks) I don't know how I'm supposed to get this done. I don't think the CIO understands what he is asking for.*

The technology leader is in a meeting with the CIO (Ajay), discussing the request.

CIO (Ajay)	We really need this done before the end of this quarter. Can you make it happen?
Technology leader (Hong)	*(Hesitates)* Uh, I'm not sure. One, it's a lot of work and, two, I don't think we should be producing a report and exporting it into an Excel spreadsheet.
CIO (Ajay)	*(Firmly)* Hong, we need this done! Can you make it happen or not?

| Technology leader (Hong) | *(Reluctantly)* Yes, we'll make it happen. |
| | *(Frustrated and thinks) I can't believe I agreed to this. There's no way we should be doing it this way.* |

We now find ourselves in a different meeting with upper management in the conference room, presenting the completed task.

| CIO (Ajay) | Well done, Hong! I knew you could do this. Everyone, that is why I love Hong – he can get anything sorted. He is our Elon! No problem is too big, is it, Hong? |
| Narrator | Hong says nothing in response, but he is aware of the technical debt that has also been delivered and the impact to his credibility within the team. In order to effectively say 'no' to upper management, leaders must first understand the reasons behind the request and assess whether it aligns with the organization's goals and objectives. |

10×Generation

If the organizational leadership has been provided with full details of the impacts of the request and still pushes forward, the responsibility sits squarely with the senior executives. The onus is on the technology leaders to educate senior stakeholders on an area in which they might lack detailed knowledge.

Agreement must be sought to revisit the technical debt in a timely manner, and to recognize the impacts that the decision has had on the delivery teams. A debt will always need to be repaid, and the senior executives need to have a clear line of sight of this.

When senior leaders are forced to make decisions with further-reaching implications, they need to revisit the organizational culture. If we see these types of pressures placed on senior-level employees, it is entirely possible that this is also happening in the lower tiers.

> *It doesn't make sense to hire smart people and then tell them what to do; we hire smart people so they can tell us what to do.*
> Steve Jobs[29]

By allowing our people to be heard, we create a virtuous cycle of enablement. Once we have this embedded, we then need to be considering the voice of the customer. In a startup or scaleup organization, we see a sharing of responsibility for the voice of the customer with product owners. As the organization grows, this must be separated out, and the customer needs to have their own representative. This can be seen in the next scene.

Act 1, Scene 8: I speak for the customer

#SMB #Enterprise #LargeEnterprise

#Operational #Tactical #Strategic

There is an area in many scaleup or SMB organizations that is misaligned or never considered, and that is the need for a VOC representative. In a startup, the product manager may believe that this is the role of product, but as the business grows, the VOC role needs to be filled in order to have an unbiased view of the customer need.

The need to have key items representing the VOC is often left behind and not considered an integral part of the product roadmap. In many organizations, we will see contention between the VOC representative and the product and technology teams. Here we see how one such interaction plays out between the VOC representative and the head of product.

Narrator	Picture the newly created role of head of VOC. Our organization has not had anyone in place to speak on behalf of the customer, and this has always fallen onto the shoulders of the head of product. Our scene is set with the head of VOC and the head of product discussing the product roadmap.
Head of VOC (Claudia)	Roberto, thanks for your time today. I really need to discuss the analysis I've completed on the latest product release and the NPS we've received.

Claudia hands Roberto a copy of the net promoter score report.

Head of product (Roberto)	This doesn't look right, Claudia. I personally helped to design those last features, and, based on the research I've performed, I think they're exactly what's needed to increase our market share.
Head of VOC (Claudia)	Roberto, I've surveyed a large selection of our customer segments, and, based on the percentage of promoters of our brand versus the percentage of detractors, I can tell you with great accuracy that the latest release did not hit the mark. I'd be really keen to see the research you did to understand what our customer wants, so that I can fold this into my own analysis going forward.
Head of product (Roberto)	I've been working at this company since we started – I think I know what our customers want, and this is what's built into our roadmap.
Head of VOC (Claudia)	I'm so glad you raised the roadmap, Roberto. I have some changes to our features that our customers have been clear they would like to see in the upcoming releases. How do I get these on the roadmap?

Head of product (Roberto)	The roadmap is completely full until next year. I've been working really hard with the senior executive to understand their priorities, and I can't see a way of changing these now. I'm sure that what we're developing will meet the customers' needs.
Head of VOC (Claudia)	I have significant data points to support the need to change some of the features in the product roadmap. I really want to take you through this so that we can come to an agreement.
Head of product (Roberto)	If you want to include elements from your findings, which feature should we de-prioritize? Which one is least important to the customer based on your research? Something has to give.
Head of VOC (Claudia)	*(Thinks about this.)* OK, Roberto, I'll discuss with the exec and see what feature they think would be least important based on the analysis and what should be de-prioritized, and I'll come back to you.
Head of product (Roberto)	Sounds good. Let me know when you want to meet up again to discuss. In future, you'll need to be involved in the product roadmap planning, Claudia, to make sure your items are included in the development cycle, otherwise we're going to have prioritization issues ongoing.
Head of VOC (Claudia)	That would be great, Roberto. Thank you.
Narrator	Now that Claudia understands what is required to get an item added to the backlog, she will raise the available options, based on the customer needs, to the executive team. With the data she has gathered, she is certain that the next features will not delight the organization's customers, and that its market share will continue to slip if action is not taken. VOC can only influence the organization's executive, but knowing that for something to be included, something else will need to drop, means that the decision will come down to what the senior executive believes is most important.

10×Generation

Here we find a newly created role that has a singular focus on the customers' needs and wants. In many small-to-medium organizations, the VOC role is filled by the marketing team or product managers, or not at all. In the 10×Generation, the customer's voice is an integral part of the delivery lifecycle.

Without clear alignment between the customer and the organization, there is a strong chance that the product will not meet the customers' needs and market share will be impacted. Understanding whether a customer is likely to promote your brand is key in retaining market share.

The solution is to bring in a VOC role *before* it becomes vital to the organization's continued growth; the leadership should consider including this role in a blended team structure. The following points provide additional actions that can be taken when considering adding VOC to your structure:

- Begin integrating the VOC function with the product and technology leadership, ensuring that the VOC reports into the same C-level leader. This will allow alignment across product, technology and VOC.
- VOC needs to take product and technology leaders on the VOC journey, explaining the importance of metrics, including:
  - Net promoter score – how this is measured, what it means, understanding customer satisfaction
  - A/B testing
  - Tracking customer themes to help build out the product roadmap
- Bring customer-centricity to the forefront to ensure that the organization's product roadmap addresses specific customer segments that other departments such as marketing, trading and customer service deem important.

Gartner says: 'NPS® alleviates challenges associated with success factors such as gaining executive support and effectively communicating the importance of customer loyalty.'[30] However, Gartner also states that many organizations are moving away from using NPS as the only measure of success.

Multiple metrics to understand customer wants and needs should be considered to ensure a well-rounded VOC experience in the organization. When we have a clear view of the customer, conversations between departments have a clearer understanding of how their actions will impact the customer's experience with the organization. Within an organization, the VOC role may be defined as a customer success role or chief experience officer, a role that is clearly focused on what the customer deems important.

Enterprise

The enterprise organization has many more departments, is multi-layered and has complicated structures that are deeply hierarchical, similar to those of the SMB but greater in complexity. The scenarios at the operational view will demonstrate the importance of open communication and the need to embed the 10×Generation principles at the foundational layer first.

Act 1, Scene 9: Never build a house of sticks – why architecture is important

#Scaleup #SMB #Enterprise #LargeEnterprise

#Operational #Tactical #Strategic

From the previous scenes that impact the SMB, we see what happens when technology leaders are not empowered to say 'no' to requests from the senior executives in an organization. This is not a new problem, and is faced at the enterprise level – but, depending on the size of an enterprise, this scenario may be taking place in many areas of the business. The little-known issue is where senior members in silos negate the expertise of peers to push for single-minded outcomes.

Education across groups becomes very challenging as organizations scale, and, in an enterprise-sized organization, it may be non-existent. If this is the case, it will require significant change management to implement. It is not impossible, but requires buy-in at all levels. When silos are created and education and empowerment is no longer a part of the organization's DNA, we see key members of teams not being taken seriously. Foundational roles become disempowered, and their input is disregarded in an effort to increase delivery.

When measures of success are at the silo level, not across the organization, we will see impacts on velocity and an increase in technical debt. Individual measures create a culture where one team's needs are placed higher than another's; we see misalignment of overall objectives and a deepening of team objectives, where teams are siloed within the organization. As the organization grows and barriers represent the new operating model, delivery slows. Let's see how this plays out.

Lights come on and we are in a conference room, filled with the sound of excited chatter as team members take their seats around the large table. A whiteboard at the front of the room is already filled with notes and ideas, and a projector is set up to display a presentation.

Senior PM   All right, everyone. Let's get started.
(Jackson)

The team members quieten down and focus their attention on Jackson.

Senior PM   As you all know, we have a tight deadline for the Johnson project.
(Jackson)   So, we need to make the most of our time today and come up with a solid plan to get it done on time.

The team members nod in agreement.

| Senior PM (Jackson) | First, let's go over the scope of the project and what needs to be done. |
| | *(Gestures to the whiteboard)* As you can see, we have a lot of tasks to complete, so we must break them down and assign them to the right people. |

The team members start discussing and making suggestions, and Jackson listens carefully, taking notes and making adjustments to the plan on the whiteboard.

Head of architecture (Cillian)	Jackson, I have some concerns about the project. The current architecture is not scalable and will not meet the long-term needs of the company.
Senior PM (Jackson)	*(Dismissively)* Yeah, yeah, we can worry about that later. Right now, we just need to get this project done on time.
Head of architecture (Cillian)	But if we don't address the architectural issues now, we'll end up wasting time and resources in the future when we have to redo the whole project.
Senior PM (Jackson)	Cillian, I appreciate your concerns, but we don't have time for that right now – the product needs this ASAP.

Six months have passed since the ambitious launch of the highly anticipated software project. The team is on a bridge call at midnight with all senior developers trying to fix a Severity 1 incident. The site reliability engineers (SREs) are busy trying to write up an incident report.

| Senior engineer (Rob) | This is a result of poor architecture decisions that were made during inception that Cillian called out. |

Next day: in the dimly lit conference room, a group of weary engineers and project managers have gathered for an emergency meeting. The air is thick with tension as the technology lead, Sarah, stands at the front of the room, her expression a mixture of frustration and exhaustion.

| Technology lead (Sarah) | *(Her voice heavy with resignation)* We all knew this was coming. |
| Software engineer (James) | Our architecture decisions have come back to haunt us. Our systems are buckling under the load, and we're seeing crashes, slow response times and, worst of all, data corruption. |

Database admin (Nancy)	I tried optimizing some of the code, but the foundational design flaws are making it nearly impossible to make any significant improvements. And the way we decided to structure our databases is causing a cascade of issues. Data integrity has been compromised, and we're losing crucial user information.

As Sarah surveys the faces in the room, she can see the exhaustion and frustration etched onto each one. The reality of their predicament is sinking in. Their rushed decisions to meet deadlines and their disregard for scalability have led them to this breaking point.

Technology lead (Sarah)	*(Her tone now one of determination)* We need to address this systematically. We can't keep putting out fires. We're going to have to make some tough choices and prioritize stability over new features for now.
Narrator	Over the next few weeks, the team embark on a gruelling journey of code refactoring, database restructuring and system redesign. They are essentially rebuilding their project from the ground up, but this time with a clear focus on long-term sustainability and scalability.

10×Generation

Enterprise architecture (EA), if done well, is the practice of adopting a comprehensive and structured approach to the design and planning of all strategic initiatives in an organization.

This includes aligning technology with business goals and strategies while ensuring that all of the organization's systems and processes are integrated and working towards a common objective. Effective EA can help an organization improve efficiency, reduce costs and better adapt to changing business needs.

Build business decisions on *data*, not people's opinions. Always use architecture decision records (ADRs) to explain the reasoning and value of why the architecture decisions were made in the first place.

Ensuring that the right frameworks are used, and that every tier and employee in the organization has been educated in the validity of each one, means that the way decisions are made will take the organization many steps closer to the 10×Generation state.

The 10×Generation embodies empowerment, adaptation, assessment and alignment, working towards a common organizational goal and a common organizational strategy. In the 10×Generation state, silos no longer exist. Each department works in harmony with the other and is educated to do so, enabling the organization to shift closer to its optimal state.

When working optimally, there is no need to divert teams to work on deliverables outside of the agreed plan. Shadow IT (or IT within separate departments) has no place; but in the following scenario we see this being proposed.

Act 1, Scene 10: Shadow IT and the infamous side project

#SMB #Enterprise #LargeEnterprise

#Operational #Strategic

Two of the challenges associated with digital transformation is to create teams without causing bottlenecks and to expand the workforce overseeing the changes without increasing the headcount. When an organization is scaling to meet demand, the notion of 'side projects' will creep in, and the side projects will create barriers within teams. If a side project is not aligned with the organization's strategy, it can derail ways of working, produce unexpected outcomes and create more work in the long term.

Here we see a side project derailing an entire delivery cycle.

It's a bright, sunny day and the team members are gathered around the table in the conference room, laptops open and papers scattered in front of them. The senior project manager, Jackson, stands at the head of the table, leaning against the whiteboard. The group looks towards Jackson.

Senior PM (Jackson)	OK, team. We've got a lot to cover today, so we need to stay focused. Let's get started on the machine learning backlog. We need to have all the models ready to go by the end of quarter 2. This deadline is rapidly approaching and the machine learning team has plenty of capacity.
Technology leader (Hong)	Wait a minute, Jackson, shouldn't we focus on getting the product requirements vetted first? I know we have the machine learning team, but aren't we being a little premature?
Senior PM (Jackson)	No, no, the machine learning roadmap is more important. We need to generate buzz in the market, and the best way to get people excited about our models is to start producing. We have to get this team working.
Technology leader (Hong)	But if our product isn't ready yet, how do we know what to include in the models? What is the business asking for? How will we measure success if we don't understand the requirements?
Senior PM (Jackson)	We'll figure it out as we go. Remember we are working in an Agile world now; this is what we learned after the last digital transformation. We need to move fast on this one.
Principal engineer (Dagmar)	Jackson, if we don't have a clear understanding of the product and its features, we could end up delivering something that doesn't meet customer needs or expectations. It doesn't matter how fast we go if we have to redo it all at the end because we missed the mark.

Senior PM (Jackson)	You heard the CEO: we have to delight the market, and machine learning is new and exciting. This was the main reason this team was brought in. If we can get this out into the wild we will be leading the pack.
Technology leader (Hong)	Jackson, is any of this work on the product roadmap? If we divert teams onto this, other work will be impacted.
Senior PM (Jackson)	Let me worry about the product roadmap. This project is important and we just need to make it work. We have a team of machine learning engineers who have significant capacity, and we need to get them working.
Narrator	The team ultimately decides to prioritize building the models and present them at the next showcase, a few months away. This is a classic scenario of putting the cart before the horse, where a solution to meet market needs is sold to the executive. Without proper planning, the team is running out of work and is yet to deliver the value as promised.

10×Generation

While side projects are great when done at a strategic level, they often fail when they are spin-off ventures to explore new ideas or opportunities that do not meet the business needs. These side projects can take many different forms, such as developing new products or services, entering into new markets or industries, or experimenting with new business models.

Side projects, if done properly, can help organizations stay innovative and adapt to changing market conditions. They can also be a way for an organization to test the feasibility of new ideas without committing significant resources to them. However, managing side projects can be challenging, as they often require balancing the needs and priorities of the main organization with the goals and objectives of the side project. It's important to carefully assess the potential risks and benefits of any side project, and to have clear strategies in place for managing and tracking progress.

There is a difference between a fully aligned side project and shadow IT. Shadow IT is the process whereby individual departments take it upon themselves to implement IT solutions to solve only their needs. Embracing the 10×Generation state, and providing visibility across the organization as to interdepartmental needs, will ensure that the use of shadow IT dissipates.

IT needs across the organization are discussed, agreed on as they meet the organization's strategic need, and then implemented with the full support of all departments – especially the IT department, which will ultimately have to support any solution.

With this level of backing across departments, we see a thriving business. In the next scenario we see what happens without it.

Act 1, Scene 11: A body of advocates versus a murder of crows

#Scaleup #SMB #Enterprise #LargeEnterprise

#Operational #Tactical #Strategic

In any organization, there is a need for business advocacy in technology, and for technology advocacy in the business. There needs to be a 'meeting of the minds' to ensure that there is alignment across the business on the importance of each individual team, and agreement on what each team needs in order to be able to deliver to the organization.

When advocacy is missing, there is an eventual misalignment of scope and responsibility, and a culture of blame can easily seep into the organization. When this starts to happen, the need for advocacy becomes more important, and it is only possible with defined accountabilities across all tiers and departments.

Our scene looks at a technology delivery function that is struggling to support an organization because the scope of deliverables is unclear.

Stage lights come up and we see a robust meeting taking place in the boardroom. The head of the enterprise project management office (EPMO) is discussing the delivery of several major projects that the organization has prioritized, and is having to deliver the bad news that the projects are going to be late.

Narrator	The organization has been developing a strong sales and marketing strategy to increase its market share. The half-yearly results were not as strong as expected, and the senior leadership agreed to innovative solutions that would show the organization's market dominance. The projects have unfortunately hit a snag, and the head of EPMO needs to recalibrate the delivery dates with the business. As we join the conversation, we see a lack of understanding between key business stakeholders as to why the projects are delayed. There is a definite blame culture, pitting technology against different departments, and this tension is impacting delivery.
Head of EPMO (Awit)	Thank you for attending the portfolio prioritization meeting. We need to address a couple of issues that have been flagged on our two major projects.
Head of sales and marketing (Hans)	What do you mean, 'issues'? This is the first time I'm being made aware of this. Although I'm not surprised, with technology having to be involved in this. We should have just contracted the outsource development company that I suggested months ago.
Head of EPMO (Awit)	Hans, I know you are distressed, but this meeting is the best place for us to work through the issues and to review scope and delivery expectations.

Head of sales and marketing (Hans)	I'm so tired of dealing with the ineptness of the technology function. How many times do we have to make our needs heard? This happens every time the technology department is engaged. This is not good enough, seriously! Whatever. Let's just get on with it.

The head of EPMO continues with the meeting and takes the business stakeholders through the portfolio.

Later that same week in a different meeting:

Head of sales and marketing (Hans)	Swaty, I am so sick and tired of the excuses from the technology department. Their delivery is woeful, and we're constrained to having to use them for everything. I think I need to speak with the CEO and get some budget to invest in my own projects.
Head of P&C (Swaty)	I totally agree with you, Hans. I cannot get anything delivered at all. It's just ridiculous. If my team delivered as much as the technology team then I would be out of a job. I don't understand why everything takes so long, and when it's delivered it doesn't meet the brief at all.
Narrator	Hans decides to take matters into his own hands and reaches out to the CEO. He wants to propose bringing in his own technology resources to deliver what he needs in his department.

Hans sets up a meeting with the CEO.

Head of sales and marketing (Hans)	Ken, this is ridiculous. We can't get anything delivered, and it's always late and of such poor quality. I want to have my own technology resources that I can manage, so I can get things done. I have budget – I just need your approval.
Narrator	The CEO listens intently to this argument, but is not convinced this is the best way forward. Hans, feeling ignored, decides to encourage all other leaders to put pressure on the CEO to do something about this. At the next portfolio meeting, the head of EPMO is swamped with criticism from all key stakeholders. The meeting is starting to turn into a debacle. The smear campaign that Hans started is taking hold, and multiple complaints are being escalated to the CEO. The meeting ends with a very flustered head of EPMO feeling quite rattled.

The CEO sets up a meeting with the head of EPMO.

CEO (Ken)	Awit, I don't think the EPMO is functioning. Delivery is poor and the quality doubly so. I have more internal complaints than I can manage. Perhaps we need to rethink the delivery strategy?
Head of EPMO (Awit)	Ken, this is all Hans' doing. He's unhappy with his project and can't see that the technology department is managing a huge portfolio of work. It has managed to increase delivery from 40% to 70% in the last eight months, but no one is recognizing this. The department leads need to work with us, not against us. We must advocate for each other, otherwise we're going to be wasting a lot of money and no one is going to be satisfied.
Narrator	The conversation ends with no resolution. The smear campaign continues, and the blame culture continues to grow.

10×Generation

In the 10×Generation state, blame and misinformation do not exist; and, thanks to the organization's adherence to the first principle, empowerment, everyone has a clear understanding of what they are accountable for. The entire department and the organization have visibility of all objectives. The change to the 10×Generation state will be achieved using an iterative approach, and this can be done only by working through the four principles. If you are working in an organization with well-entrenched ways of working, the approach will be slow and will require buy-in from all tiers of the organization.

When the organization follows the second principle, adaptation, and implements the suggested rituals (see Chapter 8), teams will have clarity of purpose and a visual display of activity, which will become the driving factor in decision-making. The main ritual that will reinforce advocacy is the 'curiosity and growth' part of this principle – most importantly, implementing curiosity *task forces*. The task forces are designed to have teams work together, think outside the box, and understand not only the potential innovations that can be made, but the priorities of all other work that the team is managing. Through walking a mile in someone else's shoes, this creates a culture of *knowing*.

Advocacy in the 10×Generation state is created when teams care about the output of others. They support each other and are determined to succeed, not at the individual or team level but organization-wide.

When an underperforming organization does not have advocacy at its core, and an understanding across the organization of what is important, there will inevitably be only one solution on offer, as we shall see in our next script.

Act 1, Scene 12: Yet another digital transformation

#SMB #Enterprise #LargeEnterprise

#Operational #Tactical #Strategic

Well, we are only half-way through this guide and have finally decided to address the elephant in the room: the dreaded digital transformation. Two words that make anyone in an organization shudder. That moment when consultants come in and advise that the only way forward is to change the technology.

In each of our scenes so far, we have covered multiple scenarios that address the structural misalignment that create bloat and impacts efficiencies. In the final scene of Act 1, we will demonstrate the digital transformation conversation that takes place. This conversation happens daily, and if you have never been impacted by it, you can consider yourself lucky.

We find ourselves in the CEO's office, where the CFO and CIO are meeting to discuss the organization's delivery performance. The stage is sparse, with a boardroom table cluttered with coffee mugs and half-full glasses of water. The projector is showing the organization's annual financials, and now the focus is on market share.

Narrator	As the organization has grown, so have its fixed costs. More employees, more physical office space and much more infrastructure. Since the heady days of being a startup, the delivery of new features to the existing product has slowed dramatically. Technical debt is growing and market share is decreasing. The CEO is feeling pressure from shareholders and a need to improve overall efficiencies. We are introduced to a leading organizational design consultant, who has the answers to the organization's concerns.
CEO (Ken)	Thank you all for coming this morning. As you can see by the current state of affairs, we are in trouble and we need to fix the problem immediately. If we don't improve our market share, we may need to consider lay-offs.

Grumbling is heard from the executives in the room.

CEO (Ken)	Ajay, I have repeatedly asked that we improve our throughput, and yet we find ourselves here once again. Our technology is ageing, and you keep telling me that the throughput is all you can achieve without more headcount.

CIO (Ajay)	That is correct, Ken. I've been requesting more headcount for months. The team simply cannot keep up with the requests that come from all avenues of the business. We're not only delivering on the product roadmap, but are also managing all the other technology needs across the business. There's no cohesion across departments, and everyone's projects are important.
CEO (Ken)	This feels like more excuses, Ajay. Throwing more people at this isn't going to resolve the problem.
CIO (Ajay)	I agree that throwing more resources at a problem doesn't help. We need better alignment across all departments. We need to be working towards a common goal instead of working in silos.
CEO (Ken)	I don't understand what you mean, Ajay; however, I have the answer to our problems. I was at a CEO summit where there were quite a few speakers and I heard this guy speak. He totally gets our problem. Let me introduce Pierre, an organizational design consultant who I have engaged to help us out.

Pierre walks into the boardroom.

Org design consultant (Pierre)	Hello all. I am Pierre, but if that's too hard, just call me Pete. I am here to help you improve on your delivery efficiencies and gain back your rightful market share. I have been in the consulting game for a long time, and I have fixed many failing organizations. Ken has explained the problem as he sees it, and I know, with my tried and tested formula, we will have you back in the game in no time.
CIO (Ajay)	OK, what are you proposing, Pierre?
Org design consultant (Pierre)	Please call me Pete. From what I can see, your organization needs to get into the 21st century. You are running old tech, haven't got the right processes in place and don't have the right structures. My business helps companies such as yours by completely transforming your tech from where you are now to a fully digital experience. In order to improve, you have to undertake a digital transformation. Your tech department needs an entire overhaul.
CEO (Ken)	That is exactly right, Pete. If we complete a digital transformation, we'll be able to deliver to the market rapidly and get this business back on track.
CIO (Ajay)	Ken, I disagree. The issue is not only with my department. I concede that we need to change some things, but there are concerns across the business. If we just focus on tech, what about everyone else? We still lack the visibility in other departments and at the executive level.

| CEO (Ken) | Ajay, I know that being singled out may seem a little harsh, but this organization needs a major overhaul, and this is what I'm here to do. Your department needs to get on the same page and make this work. Pete and his team will start on Monday. |

Ajay looks around the room dejected and walks out of the meeting.

Fast forward to six months later.

Narrator	We find ourselves back in the boardroom. Pierre and his consultants have completed the digital transformation in the technology tier. Headcount has been reduced. Additional processes have been implemented and the product roadmap has been agreed to. The tech stack is still being upgraded, which will – supposedly – continue after the consultant's departure.
Org design consultant (Pierre)	*(Presentation being displayed)* As you can see, Ken, the plan has gone really well. As projected, we've reduced headcount by 25% and we're well on track to have the tech stack uplifted. The cost for the uplift did go over what we had originally anticipated, but our tech consultants are confident that they'll finish on time, within the next six months. Once we're done, we'll exit as per the contract and leave you to it.
CEO (Ken)	This is a great update, Pete. It is great to have a project delivered on time.

Twelve months later (when it should have been six) and the consultants have left.

| Narrator | The reduced headcount has impacted the team's ability to successfully undertake handover. Various departments are still pressuring the technology department to support and implement new technology solutions, and, with the digital transformation, some of the requirements for departments are now no longer possible, as they were not considered in the project. The CIO needs to employ more people to manage the new technology, and bring the consultants back in to assist with overall support, as handover was not possible. Costs have escalated, and product delivery is now impacted further, as the transformation has had flow-on effects on the product roadmap. |
| CEO (Ken) | Ajay, I don't understand. We're still behind on the product roadmap, we're not delivering, and the headcount is higher than before we did the transformation. How is this possible? |

CIO (Ajay)	The individual departments weren't considered as part of the uplift, and now we're managing requests that we can't meet. With the headcount reductions, we haven't been able to keep up with the maintenance and support, so we've needed to hire more people. With the implications of the new tech stack, we needed more people. It's as simple as that.

10×Generation

When the needs of all departments are not considered in a digital transformation, it is never going to deliver the promised outcomes.

In the 10×Generation state, all departments are looped into any changes that will have a substantial impact on the organization. Decisions are made as a collective, with all inputs understood. Processes that benefit everyone are refined, implemented and successfully embedded before a milestone is considered achieved.

To stop the never-ending roundabout of digital transformations, the core understanding of what is needed across the entire organization is fully mapped out. It is architected to deliver across all departments and then embarked upon.

The key thing to remember is that digital transformations are sold to executives and filled with promises that, on the surface, appear to have been met. The reality is that if other departments are not considered in the overall transformation, some areas will be misunderstood, alignment will be impacted; and as the support to all, IT will take the brunt of the failed project.

Act 1 has covered the operational view, and has demonstrated how not working in the ultimate state can derail your organization – no matter what size it is, or where you are in organizational growth and maturity. This misalignment will permeate all tiers of an organization, and will now be continued into the tactical tier.

Act 2: The silent sins of scaling

In Act 2 we look into the issues being faced at a tactical or departmental level in an organization, which in the 10×Generation state is known as the *tactical* view (see Figure 18). In this tier we will see each of the main challenges discussed at length. When an organization expands, it is in the tactical view that the growth, if left unchecked, will create significant swell and experience unproductive silos. Many departments that you recognize will be represented in the upcoming scripts.

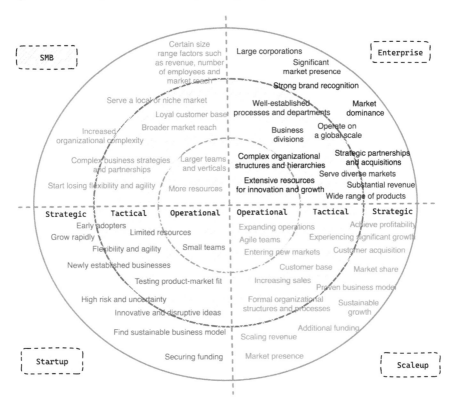

Figure 18 Radius of growth: The tactical layer

The difference between the operational view and the tactical view, when an organization is struggling with uncontrolled growth, is that in the operational view this will inevitably lead to the need for a digital transformation. In the tactical view, when the digital transformation is announced, it has very little impact on the tactical departments, except for a deterioration in technical support during the transformation phase.

The impact of each challenge is felt in the tactical view when the organization's performance is not meeting financial commitments and it is not achieving, or is losing, market share. For many organizations that are heavy in the middle tier, this is the first place where change will be focused. The view of the tactical tier is that of surplus, not of need, and will be targeted first.

Setting the tactical scene

In this second act, we are introduced to new characters, and will also see some already familiar faces as each scene plays out. As in Act 1, we will be revisiting each organizational type: startup or scaleup, SMB and enterprise. Each scenario builds on the key challenges that an organization will encounter, but from the view of individual departments.

Startup or scaleup

In the startup or scaleup scenario, we are given scenes that show how the middle tier faces its challenges in the growth phase of an organization. As the departments try to find their place in the world, they face the friction created when balancing needed growth and perceived inefficiencies. In our first scene, we find ourselves watching the endless debate over whether to use an insource or an outsource model.

Act 2, Scene 1: Out-sorcery

#Startup #Scaleup #SMB #Enterprise #LargeEnterprise

#Tactical #Strategic

Many of you who have worked in any organization will have been faced with the insource/outsource dance that leaders often grapple with. In the constant quest to save costs, organizations will look to outsourcing. However, going into this without all the information needed can result in disastrous consequences, such as those we will see in our first scene.

Our scene opens with the head of finance, head of customer service and customer service manager discussing whether or not to outsource the customer service department to another country.

Narrator	When an SMB begins to experience bloat and has unmanaged fixed costs, the standard course of action is to look at outsourcing to reduce headcount and reduce fixed costs.
	For many years there has been the argument that outsourcing creates more problems for a business, as you lose the control that you have when internal resources do the work.
Head of finance (Chien)	Krish, we need to reduce costs across all departments. We've grown too fast, and it's been uncontrolled. We need to reduce headcount, and each department needs to look at ways that this can be done.

Head of customer service (Krish)	I understand what we need to do, Chien, but I still have a service that needs to be offered to our customers. I've been working with Petra on this, and we think we have an option, but we need to run it past you first.
Customer service manager (Petra)	Chien, we are looking at outsourcing a big chunk of the customer services team to a cheaper location.
	I estimate that if we shift headcount overseas, we could save significantly on salaries and still provide our customers with a good service.
Head of finance (Chien)	What are you proposing for your onshore headcount?
Head of customer service (Krish)	If we make some roles redundant and let others leave through natural attrition, we won't achieve the savings this year, but we will in the following year.
Customer service manager (Petra)	We do need to consider departmental morale during this process. We can't have customer service call metrics impacted while we make the transition.
Head of customer service (Krish)	Also, there is a lot of work to outsource. We need to develop the scripts, train the outsource agency and trial this for a while.
Head of finance (Chien)	So, this is not a silver bullet is what I am hearing, but if we get this right, we could save a lot of money?
Head of customer service (Krish)	Exactly. So, what do you think, Chien? Should we proceed?
Head of finance (Chien)	We need to save the money, so let's get onto this – but keep it quiet. As you said, we don't want people panicking until we're ready to transition.
Narrator	The business made the decision to outsource all of its customer service teams to another country with cheaper operating costs.
	However, the cost of change, and of the ongoing management of the outsource vendor, has exceeded the costs originally anticipated.
	The service being provided to customers is not meeting any of the agreed metrics.

It's been a few months, and the head of customer service is being grilled by the CEO and the CFO.

CEO (Ken)	Krish, we have a real problem with this outsource model.
	We're getting more and more complaints about our customer service and we have no fallback. The cost savings haven't been realized, as it's costing more to manage the outsourcing. The service levels in place don't have clearly defined measures of success, and there's no underperformance compensation in the contract.
	This is a mess.
Head of customer service (Krish)	I know it is, Ken, and I am sorry.
	I thought that outsourcing was the right thing for the business, but we just can't get the balance right with the outsource vendor. We need a bit more time and money to really land this.
Head of finance (Chien)	Krish, you said you had this in hand. We needed to save money and now we're in a worse situation. Who's managing the outsourcer?
Head of customer service (Krish)	We've left this up to the outsource company. They have their people in place to lead, but I guess this is a problem in itself.
	I never should have let Petra go. She said this would happen and I didn't listen.

Our scene ends without an acceptable resolution.

10×Generation

Outsourcing has always been thought of as the best way to reduce costs and keep internal headcount down. Instead of looking at departmental structures, processes and ways of working, it always seems cheaper to offload the problem to an outsourcer.

The issue with this is that, wherever the headcount resides, if the processes and ways of working are not clearly defined, there will always be cost and quality implications.

To reduce departmental excess, the 10×Generation principles will provide a roadmap to deliver the savings that the business is calling for. In the optimal state, outsourcing is not always the solution. The decision points are more considered, as the organization is not suffering from bloat and therefore the cost-saving implications are not necessarily a variable to be included.

Embedding the first principle, empowerment, will provide clearly defined accountabilities for each role in the department.

Through the fourth principle, alignment, comes process improvement, and greater visibility of potential gaps and duplication of effort, giving clear indications of where bottlenecks are forming in the department. If the business chooses to outsource an entire function, it can easily do so once the work to document the first principle is complete.

In the 10×Generation state, there is room for either insourcing and outsourcing; however, this can be achieved successfully only when processes and accountabilities are clearly defined and understood by all.

It is also important to realize that whether the business insources or outsources, there is always a level of business leadership that is needed. Leadership can never be outsourced; it must always remain within, and align with, strategic intent and a focus on working cohesively across all departments.

Working together is key to the 10×Generation state. When this is not achieved, we see friction and assumptions taking control of the operating model. When there is no clarity, we see agitation becoming commonplace, leading to multiple friction points being felt.

Act 2, Scene 2: Dealing with the scattergun approach

#Startup #Scaleup #SMB #Enterprise #LargeEnterprise

#Tactical #Strategic

In many organizations, discrepancies often exist between those who are responsible for an activity and those who are not. When assumptions are made, we often find expectations not being met. In the next scene we see what happens when there is a disconnect between who is responsible for data insights and who is not. We see what the scattergun approach from senior leadership does to fix a problem. Instead of bringing the team together, we find ourselves in a place of assumption and accusation – always an unproductive place for a team to be.

The business intelligence (BI) team is being held accountable for the mismatch of data that the finance team is expecting. The reporting outputs are not showing consistent information, and the finance team doesn't understand why the BI team cannot seem to get this right. We find a senior stakeholder escalating an issue that they are unclear about, and that their team was directly responsible for. This type of deflection creates angst in other teams and impacts the senior stakeholder's credibility.

We find ourselves in our head of business intelligence's home office. He is glued to his computer monitor, scrolling through something on screen. He is looking very distressed and making notes on his notepad next to his keyboard.

Narrator	When we have a disconnect between departments, we see friction created and additional work layered on already pressured team members.
	When deliverables are missed and accountability is not being taken, it causes a flow-on effect across departments.
	We hear a call come through to the head of business intelligence on Zoom.
Head of finance (Chien)	Hiroshi, what's going on with the BI reports that your team is meant to be delivering to the tax office? If we don't get these sent through by close of business, we're going to be in breach, which will mean we'll be fined significantly.
Head of business intelligence (Hiroshi)	I am aware of the consequences of not getting the reports in on time, Chien, and the team are working on it.
Head of finance (Chien)	You've had weeks to get this right. I don't understand what the problem is here. My team has been going through the data and it's all wrong. What is happening?
Head of business intelligence (Hiroshi)	Chien, we've been working with your team on the data rules for weeks to ensure that this is right. We've configured them as per the requirements. Is it possible something was missed with the requirements? We sent through the reports last week for confirmation of the data and received the all-clear from your team.
Head of finance (Chien)	Well, I don't know what you're seeing, but my guys are telling me the data is all wrong. Obviously your team haven't interpreted the requirements correctly. You need to fix this immediately.
Head of business intelligence (Hiroshi)	Chien, we can only look at the rules that have been provided. If these are correct, then the data being produced is correct.
	Your team signed this off. My team isn't responsible for the data – that comes from the source systems. We're only responsible for configuring the reports based on the rules you provide.
Head of finance (Chien)	Well, it needs to be fixed, and I am holding you responsible. I'm emailing the CEO, CFO and head of compliance about this.

Chien disconnects from the call.

Narrator	Hiroshi looks distressed, but he knows he is right. He cannot be held accountable for the incoming data and the resulting outputs, can he?
	Hiroshi decides to reach out to other members of Chien's team, and contacts them for support and assistance with getting the report details sorted out.

Hiroshi calls the finance lead.

Head of business intelligence (Hiroshi)	Hello, Katie – how are you?
Finance lead (Katie)	I'm OK, Hiroshi. I need to get Chien off the warpath on these reports, that's for sure.
Head of business intelligence (Hiroshi)	Katie, I think this should be a joint effort between finance and BI. This will ensure ownership and agreement between all parties. Otherwise, we're going to have the same issues arise over and over again.
Finance lead (Katie)	I agree, but we need to get Chien to agree. You know how she can get when the pressure is on. It's always someone else's fault. Have you seen the latest email she's sent to the senior execs about this?
Head of business intelligence (Hiroshi)	I must have missed it. Let me check now.

Hiroshi reads the email and looks more distressed.

Head of business intelligence (Hiroshi)	Oh, wow. Chien is saying we've sent through incorrect data to the regulators already, when this isn't the case. I don't understand why she would do that. Is she targeting me or something?
Finance lead (Katie)	Don't worry, Hiroshi. Chien always does this – making things sound worse than they are, to get people to drop everything and work on what she believes is most important.
Head of business intelligence (Hiroshi)	Look, we have to work together, otherwise this will keep on happening. I'll reach out to Chien and seek agreement to have our departments work more closely together.

The scene ends with agreement between Katie and Hiroshi but still no agreement from Chien.

Lights dim, fade to black.

10×Generation

In immature organizations such as startups and scaleups, there is a lack of accountability and responsibility. Assumptions become the way of operating, creating a culture where accountabilities are unclear. When objectives are based on assumptions, stakeholders will always be disappointed with the outcomes.

The 10×Generation state and the embedding of the four key principles will alleviate the issues with accountability and responsibility. Many organizations will resort to the use of a RACI (a chart that categorizes parties into 'responsible', 'accountable', 'consulted' and 'informed'). The issue with the common RACI chart is that it often goes unused; individuals tend to ignore it, leading to a disconnect.

Embedding the first principle, empowerment, and being clear about what every role is accountable for and how it interfaces with other roles, thus creating visibility across the organization, will ensure accountabilities are clear and remove assumptions from the workplace.

The empowerment principle removes assumptions of task-related outcomes, and ensures that the organization's ways of working are based on agreed requirements, ownership of deliverables and accountability for decision-making. This removes the need for escalation emails and the constant dobbing-in[31] of other employees.

When the culture has been addressed, it is far easier to work towards strategic goals to help the organization gain greater market share and improve financial stability. With financial stability comes the ability to focus on product advancement and greater delivery. Understanding agility and how this improves delivery means getting closer to an ideal state, and is demonstrated in our next scene.

Act 2, Scene 3: The MVP advantage – how to not prematurely scale

#Startup #Scaleup #SMB #Enterprise #LargeEnterprise

#Tactical #Strategic

You probably know what MVP stands for – and no, it's not 'maximum valued product' or 'most valued placeholder'. Though we like the latter, as it has a tongue-in-cheek idea of the acronym highlighting the fact that an MVP may not be the most polished or complete product, but can still be highly valuable in terms of its ability to guide the product department and its investments. *Minimum viable product* as a concept has been very useful, but can become highly problematic if we scale much too early, wasting time and resources on something the organization never needed.

> *The scene starts with the head of technology (Mike) sitting alone in the office, staring at his computer screen. He looks stressed and overwhelmed.*

Narrator	The senior leadership has been sold on the dream of an MVP, whereas the product team is planning a 'Fake MVP' approach!
	In this approach, the product team launches a product that looks like an MVP, but is actually a fully featured product in disguise. This approach is taken to bypass the limitations of budget or timeline, but it can be harmful to the overall product development process because it skips the critical feedback loop that an MVP is designed to provide.

Roberto bursts into the room.

Head of product (Roberto)	Mike, I need to know how much longer until the MVP is ready to go?
Head of technology (Mike)	Roberto, I'm working as fast as I can, but we need to make sure we get this right. Rushing the MVP could lead to errors and a poor user experience.
Head of product (Roberto)	I understand your concerns, Mike, but we need to get this product out to the market as soon as possible. Our competitors are already ahead of us.
Head of technology (Mike)	I agree, but we can't lose sight of the fact that the MVP is just that – a minimum viable product. It needs to be simple and focused, or we risk creating a bloated product that no one wants.
Head of product (Roberto)	But we also need to make sure we have enough features to attract users. We can't just release a bare-bones MVP and hope for the best.
Head of technology (Mike)	I see your point, but we need to prioritize features based on their importance and impact. We can't just add everything we think is important.

Dagmar, the principal engineer, looks concerned overhearing the conversation.

Head of technology (Mike)	Roberto, we need to be careful with how we scale the product. We should focus on answering the specific question our MVP was designed to answer. If we start adding too many features, we'll lose sight of that goal.
Head of product (Roberto)	Exactly, and we need to stay ahead of the competition! I've already promised the CEO what we're building, and the marketing team has already spent a lot on promoting the product.

They agree to disagree; the lights fade out.

Narrator	The product department wins, and it starts working on adding the new features to the product.
	However, the new features are causing issues and delays, and customers start to complain about the product's reliability. As a result, the company starts losing customers and revenue. The team belatedly realizes that it has prematurely scaled the product without proper testing and validation.
	The team goes back to the drawing board to try to fix the issues, but it's too late. The damage has been done, and the company's reputation has been tarnished.

10×Generation

The 10×Generation approach ensures faster feedback and continuous improvements. The idea behind an MVP is to create a product that is simple and cost-effective to develop, yet is still valuable enough to attract customers and provide meaningful feedback for future iterations. The MVP approach helps to reduce the risk of investing significant time and resources in a product that may not be successful in the market.

Once an MVP has been launched, it isn't a case of 'one-and-done'. Feedback is gathered from early adopters, and changes are made based on that feedback. This iterative process continues until the product reaches a point where it is fully functional and meets the needs of the target market. 'Fully functional' means also removing the technical debt that was accumulated at the start due to planning a quick prototype.

Overall, it's important for all departments and executives to remember that the MVP approach should be used to gather feedback and inform future development, rather than as a shortcut or a way to bypass critical steps in the product development process.

The misunderstanding of the MVP concept in the Agile framework has created a distrust of this approach and tarnished the power of iteration. When all stakeholders and all tiers in an organization have embraced the 10×Generation approach, it creates a virtuous cycle of feedback between business and technology. This feedback enables organizations to balance demands while managing constraints. Without this foundation of open communication, we see the impacts that constraints have on an organization.

Act 2, Scene 4: Demands over priorities – a balancing act

#Startup #Scaleup #SMB #Enterprise #LargeEnterprise

#Tactical #Strategic

Startups most often have limited resources, which can create competition for funding, staff and other resources between departments. There is a balance between external and internal demands, which must be addressed, otherwise this can lead to friction and conflict as departments vie for a larger share of the available pie.

One of the most common challenges is the act of navigating the external and internal customer relationships and successfully meeting expected resource demands.

We see a group of executives and managers sitting in a large conference room, discussing the organization's roadmap for the upcoming quarter.

The room is filled with whiteboards and charts outlining the company's various departments and initiatives. Oleg, the head of IT operations, is leading the meeting. He's discussing the challenges the company is facing in managing the increasing demand for both operational technology (OpsTech) and marketing technology (MarTech).

Head of IT ops (Oleg)	As you can see from the roadmap, we have a lot of initiatives lined up for the upcoming quarter. However, we're struggling to balance the demands for both OpsTech and MarTech.
Head of sales and marketing (Hans)	I understand your concerns, Oleg, but we can't delay our marketing initiatives. Our customer-facing products must take priority.
Head of IT ops (Oleg)	I understand that, Hans, but we can't neglect our operations and infrastructure either. If we don't invest in OpsTech, we risk losing efficiency and productivity across the organization.
Head of sales and marketing (Hans)	But our marketing initiatives are crucial to driving revenue and growth. We can't afford to delay them.
Head of technology (Mike)	Can I jump in here? I'm not saying we delay anything, but we need to be realistic about what we can deliver in a given timeframe. We can't take on too much and risk impacting the quality of our work.
Head of sales and marketing (Hans)	I understand that, but we need to be aggressive in our marketing strategy. We need to stay ahead of the competition.
Head of technology (Mike)	I agree, but we also need to make sure we're building a strong foundation for our technology infrastructure. We can't ignore the importance of OpsTech.

Narrator	The two continue to argue, with other executives and managers chiming in with their opinions.
	However, as the meeting continues, it becomes clear that the organization is struggling to manage the increasing demand for both OpsTech and MarTech and without a clear strategic direction the meeting will never have a resolution that meets the organization's needs.
	The meeting ends, but the challenges of managing the external and internal customers continue.

10×Generation

The 10×Generation state prescribes that every organization has a framework such as the Eisenhower Matrix,[32] Value vs. Effort Matrix[33] or ICE (Impact, Confidence and Ease) Framework[34] to prioritize initiatives based on their impact, effort required and feasibility.

Make sure the initiatives align with the organization's overall strategy and vision. This will help you prioritize the initiatives that will have the most significant impact on the organization's long-term success (irrespective of internal or customer-facing requirements). Continuously evaluate the roadmap, and adjust it as needed based on changing priorities, new information, and feedback from customers and stakeholders.

One of the biggest reasons for failing to have the right balance is a lack of *communication* and *transparency*:

- Communicate the resource constraints and limitations to the stakeholders and customers
- Be transparent about the challenges you are facing, and work collaboratively to find solutions that will work for everyone.

In the tactical tier in startup- or scaleup-sized organizations, we see a lot of disconnects, where the foundations are not firmly in place. Without these, we see what happens as the organization grows into an SMB. Disconnection and misalignment continue to grow, and are addressed with human capital instead of by fixing the problem at the source.

Small-to-medium business

In the SMB organization, we start to see significant inflation and silos affecting the tactical tier. Each department works independently, and this, if left unchecked, will continue to grow the middle layer of the organization. We start to see the cracks show in the SMB as it grows faster than the processes can manage with. Ways of working stay the same from the scaleup phase, and the manual activities are performed by human capital.

Each department creates layers of hierarchical dependence, and this requires additional headcount to manage. The SMB, if left to its own devices, will continue to grow further away from the 10×Generation state. Having more silos within and across departments impacts visibility and organizational cohesion.

In each of the following scenes we see how the challenges affect the SMB organization.

Act 2, Scene 5: Short-term thinking leads to long-term problems

#SMB #Enterprise #LargeEnterprise

#Tactical #Strategic

In many organizations, when headcount reduction becomes the only answer to better fiscal performance, the decision-making is made based on financial factors, including salaries, deliverables and the performance of the team. The key factor that is often overlooked is what would be impacted, or what would break, if an individual or team were removed.

In the current climate, we have seen what is happening to social media giants when they cut significant numbers to turn performance around: the platform loses its credibility, and slowly loses customers and market share. In the next scenario, we see financial pressures impacting departmental cohesion, where leaders are expected to decide on who should stay and who should go.

The curtain rises and lights come up in a dimly lit meeting room, late in the evening.

We find our CEO and CFO working side by side discussing the organization's financial performance. Things are not dire, but there are opportunities to make the organization more efficient.

CEO (Ken)	Lakshmi, I think we need to look at tightening the belt. The numbers aren't terrible, but we could be doing better, and I don't want to be in a bad state at the end of the financial year without having tried to address profit margins earlier.
CFO (Lakshmi)	I agree, Ken. We need to act now.
	I've looked at some of the teams in the business that are just not delivering, and I think we should look at either cutting them completely or at least removing the higher-salaried employees.

CEO (Ken)	We do have quite a few tech team members who are on extremely high salaries, and I think if we cut some of those we would be in a better situation.
Narrator	After making arbitrary decisions on cutting headcount without consultation, the organization may be in for a nasty shock when the reductions take place.

Two weeks later, we find the head of people and culture (P&C), the CFO and the CIO meeting to discuss a reduction in the IT operations team. A decision has been made to remove the middle-management layer to save costs, and the CIO is now being informed. Not consulted, but informed.

CFO (Lakshmi)	Ajay, we need to reduce the middle-management layer in the IT operations space. You have quite a lot of headcount, and Ken wants us to find some savings.
CIO (Ajay)	All of those are more than 'just' middle managers. The IT operations team are all hands-on. They may have leadership titles, but each has a specific skill set and all are needed.
	If you start cutting the technical leadership layer out of the team, then you put this business at risk.
CFO (Lakshmi)	We really don't think so, Ajay. You have a large team of junior and mid-level team members; you should be able to make it work with that.
Head of P&C (Swaty)	Lakshmi, if we make these roles redundant, we will have difficulty rehiring if the need arises down the track.
CFO (Lakshmi)	We must make hard decisions for the good of the company, and Ken is aware of the employment laws in this region.
CIO (Ajay)	I want to speak with Ken. This is not the right course of action, and I am against it. At which point was someone going to discuss this with me and not just tell me what would happen?
Narrator	The CIO meets with the CEO but is told the same thing. The names of the individuals who will go are based on salary alone, and this is the direction the business is going in.
	The decision is made, and the redundancies take place.

Fast forward three months. The CEO meets with his senior leadership team to announce the start of buyout discussions. We find ourselves in the boardroom with the CEO, CFO, CIO, head of P&C, and chief marketing officer (CMO).

CEO (Ken)	Hello, I am pleased to announce that the UK part of the business has been successfully acquired by a large competitor in the EU.
	This will mean our share options will all vest, and we all stand to make significant profit from this.
	I cannot thank you all enough for the work you have done to make this possible. Now, over to Ajay and the tech team to work on the separation. Ajay, this will sit squarely on your shoulders, as you and your IT operations team will be integral to this process.
CIO (Ajay)	Ken, we have a problem here.
CEO (Ken)	What problem? You provided the timings you needed six months ago when we were working through the due diligence. You have the time; we just need you to get cracking.
CIO (Ajay)	Do you recall when you removed all my middle-management layer in the operations team – three months ago?
	None of us thought the acquisition would take place, and the decision to remove key team members was made as a short-term fix to the financial issues.
	Well, we have managed, only just, to keep the lights on. We haven't been able to transition knowledge from the key people that we let go, and we no longer have the internal knowledge to separate the business.
CEO (Ken)	How could you let this happen, Ajay? It's your job to run the technology function.
	Well, what are we going to do now?
CIO (Ajay)	We're going to have to try to get some of the talent back, if we can, but it's going to cost us.
Narrator	Our scene ends with a realization of the flow-on effects of poorly made decisions, made from a single lens. Short-term thinking produced a short-term solution with long-term side effects.

10×Generation

In the 10×Generation state, all roles – including their complexity, how they interface with each other, and the importance of each role – are clear to everyone in the organization. This is embedded in the first principle, empowerment. Decisions are not made in isolation but rather in consultation. The talent in the organization, and how each role interlinks with others, is known and mapped out.

If the organization is not making a profit, decisions need to be made from a place of knowledge. All factors are considered before the decision to reduce headcount is made. The roles that are deemed less important are analysed before being removed.

In the 10×Generation state, there is far less waste; therefore before a role is hired, the necessity for the role, and exactly what it is intended to do, are understood. Agreement to the hire is achieved through consultation across the team and the tiers that it would impact.

When roles are clearly defined, we find harmony across teams. When there is visibility of individual deliverables and team outcomes are understood, a workplace is much more efficient. When roles are filled with ambiguity, we give the empire builder an avenue to make their way into the organization. Once the empire builder is firmly entrenched, we see the damage that can be caused and the impacts this has on team health.

Act 2, Scene 6: Nero fiddled while Rome burned – managing empire builders

#Startup #Scaleup #SMB #Enterprise #LargeEnterprise

#Operational #Tactical #Strategic

When leaders are afraid to make the necessary changes and instead applaud the empire builders in the business, it affects more than just one person – it affects the entire team and can have a flow-on effect on the entire department and beyond. An empire builder will often want to take over areas of accountability that are owned by other teams. They will do this even if they do not have the requisite level of expertise, and will often say that they are only doing what is best for the business. The empire builder's actions have a significant impact on the cohesion of the teams that surround them.

This scenario relates to Jim Collins' 'seat on the bus' principle.[35] By mismanaging these types of employees, leaders send the wrong message across the team. Every seat on the bus is important, and an empire builder thinks only of themselves and not the health of the team, the department or the business.

Narrator	It is that time of the year when organizations are asking their employees to do 'yet another engagement survey'.
	One of the favourite questions that most such surveys have is 'Do you think that our organization / your manager is managing team well-being and that this is a great place to work?'
	All departments have received their scores, and the technology department's scores don't look good.

The CTO, Jane, is sitting in the boardroom with all of her direct reports. She is trying to set up the TV to share the slides from the survey results with the room and the people who have dialled in from home to the meeting.

CTO (Jane)	Does anyone know how I can share my slides? Oleg, when will we actually have the equipment in our boardroom working? Every time I'm in this room with senior leadership, they think it's my fault.
Head of IT ops (Oleg)	Hey Jane – I'm sorry, I was told that this was fixed last week. Not sure what's going on here.
CTO (Jane)	That's exactly how I feel looking at the engagement results – our team has scored the lowest on a few questions.
	The one that I would like to highlight and have some actions on, before we walk out of this room, is the one that says 'Do you think that our organization / your manager is managing team well-being and that this is a great place to work?'
Head of technology (Mike)	How bad does it look? And can we get individual team breakdown?
CTO (Jane)	If your team has more than five people, the answer is yes. And it looks really bad!
Head of product (Roberto)	Let's break the suspense, please.
CTO (Jane)	We got a score of 2 out of 10, when the company average is 8.

Gasps are heard, as this score is very low and is a direct reflection of mismanagement.

Head of technology (Mike)	I'm guessing this shouldn't come as a surprise – we have an employee who is struggling to stay in their lane. We know who we're talking about, and their actions are really starting to impact multiple teams across the tech organization. Boardroom kit as a case in point!
	The kit was supposed to be fixed months ago, but the lead in this space is too busy trying to grow his empire and take on more and more work from other teams. He simply hasn't focused on what he's meant to be doing.
	This activity is impacting other teams and really starting to cause problems.

Head of product (Roberto) sighs.

CTO (Jane)	Who is the senior leader here? What are they doing to curb this behaviour?

Head of technology (Mike)	It's Asim, and he has been trying.
CTO (Jane)	Well, this needs to stop!
Head of technology (Mike)	The problem is that this person's behaviour is applauded by some of the senior board members, and this makes it increasingly hard for Asim to make any changes, Jane.
CTO (Jane)	If this isn't addressed, we're going to start seeing resignations, and in this current climate we can't withstand this.
	Mike, you're going to have to support Asim on this one. We need a plan of action that we can take to the people and culture team and look at the best way of addressing this.

With a possible plan to address this particular issue and the other issues raised, the meeting concludes. We then see a conversation between the head of infrastructure (Asim) and IT operations engineer (Joey).

IT ops engineer (Joey)	Asim, you have to do something about Javiar. He works in networking and knows nothing about engineering. I don't understand how he can now own release management. This is completely outside of his remit.
	He's now telling the engineers what they can release into production. This is crazy.
Head of infrastructure (Asim)	Let me speak with him.
Narrator	Asim doesn't address the issue as he is afraid that Javiar will leave. This inaction causes more disharmony.

We see our CTO (Jane) and head of technology (Mike) meeting in Jane's office.

Head of technology (Mike)	So, we've lost another engineer. They're complaining about the release process and how it's over-burdensome.
CTO (Jane)	That doesn't make sense – what's happening there? We have a release manager who deals with this.
Head of technology (Mike)	It appears that Javiar is owning releases now, and has the release manager working as an admin for releases.
CTO (Jane)	*(Angry)* How is this possible? This needs to stop. I need to get the people and culture team onto this immediately.

As the situation with Javiar continues to spiral, the CTO raises the issue with the CEO.

CTO (Jane)	Ken, we have a problem with Javiar.
CEO (Ken)	Javiar? That doesn't sound right. He's one of our best performers. He's always here working, works over weekends, puts in more effort than anyone in his team. We'd be lost without him.
	I was thinking we should be promoting him to 'head of', as he's such an outstanding contributor.
	Last week he met with me to take me through some of his thinking to improve other departments. He's a real mover and shaker.
CTO (Jane)	That's our problem, Ken. Javiar is pushing into multiple departments, outside of his area of expertise, and is destabilizing them.
	He thinks he has the technical skills but he really doesn't. Because he has the senior execs' backing, he just pushes his way into other areas.
	His actions are prohibitive to this organization's growth plans, and he needs to either focus on his own area and get it working, or leave the business.
CEO (Ken)	It would be a shame to lose him, but it's your team. Do what you believe is best.
Narrator	Our scene ends with our CTO extremely angry at the loss of more talent from the organization because of the empire builder, but pleased that the CEO sees that this activity is detrimental to ongoing growth.

10×Generation

Regardless of whether an employee is performing or underperforming, they must be held accountable for their areas of expertise. There is a balance that must be met while working across an organization. Empire builders cannot be allowed to encroach on other areas under the guise of working in the organization's best interests. They must be able to collaborate across functions rather than try to take ownership of them.

Supporting leaders to enable them to have challenging conversations is the first step when dealing with employees. No one likes to have hard conversations – but they must be had, otherwise significant consequences will be felt across all tiers of the organization.

Things to consider when managing an empire builder (EB):

- If you want to undertake a performance improvement process, stick to the facts of the performance that are impacting the teams. Do not be conned by the 'I am doing what is best for the business' argument. They are not. They are doing what is best for them, by trying to increase their control, only thinking of themselves and their own career aspirations

- The EB will have cultivated loyalty with the C-suite leaders. They will have been in the organization for quite some time, and will feel secure in their position and the relationships they have built. You will need to get the C-suite on board when managing the EB

- EBs like to catastrophize issues and make it seem that they are the only ones who can fix them. Senior executives will be swayed by them and feel uncomfortable if you want to remove the EB

- Finally, there is the sunken cost fallacy,[36] which relates to the amount of customer or system knowledge the EB has amassed. This will need to be transitioned and this will need to be done quickly.

Ultimately getting rid of an EB has a much bigger intangible cost saving than just the monetary figures that most leaders focus on. If their way of working can be changed so that they become a team player, this will be a win-win for the organization and is the far better outcome.

By tapping into the 'WIIFM' (what's in it for me) argument, you can turn an EB around. In the 10×Generation state, this starts with clear accountability and embedding of the first and second principles: empowerment and adaptation. This can ensure that empire building never starts, and if it is already entrenched in your organization, the principles will help to re-align the EB as to the future expectations under the new way of operating.

Decisions to remove or performance-manage an EB will have impacts, and will eventually have a positive effect on the organization. When staff members are kept in the dark about decisions, however, this can have a similar effect on team cohesion to that of an EB. Trusting in your team to be able to manage with organizational changes and with progression is a key pillar in the 10×Generation state.

Here we see what happens when leadership does not trust the team it leads, and manages via fear. The situation is made worse, and ultimately the organization pays for it.

Act 2, Scene 7: The mushroom principle

#Scaleup #SMB #Enterprise #LargeEnterprise

#Operational #Tactical #Strategic

When there is misalignment between strategic and tactical tiers, we see impacts on departmental morale and mistrust of senior leadership impacting an organization's growth potential. The lack of visibility creates rumours, which, whether true or not, will create significant noise and distraction. This is often seen as mushroom management,[37] where leaders keep decision-making to themselves and the workers feel that they are being kept in the dark.

In this scenario, we find ourselves in the unenviable position of the head of finance, who has been instructed by the CEO and CFO to curb spending and reduce fixed costs across all departments. Half-yearly figures have been unfavourable, and the business needs to improve market share before it heads into a revenue-raising activity.

We find ourselves in the CFO's office as the decision is made to curb spending.

Narrator	When an organization needs to curb spending but the reasoning is not clear to the department heads, we see serious implications for morale, and the rumour mill beginning to take over, impacting delivery across departments.
CFO (Lakshmi)	Ken, based on the half-yearly figures we really need to turn things around – otherwise when we're needing to revenue raise later in the year, we're going to have difficulties showing our growth outcomes to our potential investors.
CEO (Ken)	Yeah, I get it, Lakshmi, we're going to have to curb our overall spend until our EBITDA improves enough to build confidence in the market.
CFO (Lakshmi)	Chien, what implications will this have?
Head of finance (Chien)	We'll need to discuss it with each department and get them across the cost savings measures we need to do.
	In the first instance, we should pause non-started projects, pause new hires and possibly pause backfill hires too.
CEO (Ken)	I don't want to spook people into thinking we're in financial difficulty, so perhaps we just speak to specific departments and keep this quiet.
	Just speak to the people and culture team, and tell them to go slow on backfills and new hires. Speak to the EPMO and tell them to pause new projects.

CFO (Lakshmi)	Do you think it's wise not to fill in all departments, Ken? People will talk and things could get out of hand.
CEO (Ken)	I think if we let everyone know, we'll start a stampede. Where there's smoke, there's fire, and that's the last thing we need.
CFO (Lakshmi)	Chien, I'll leave this with you.

During the following day, Chien has meetings with the heads of P&C (Swaty) and EPMO (Awit).

Head of finance (Chien)	Thank you both for joining me. I've been having meetings with Ken and Lakshmi, and have been advised that we need to reduce some costs in the business.
	From a people and culture perspective, we will need to pause any new hires, and for the backfills we need to go slow. For all new hire requests, we need to ensure we have a robust business case.
	From the EPMO perspective, we need to pause all non-essential projects and hold any projects that haven't started yet. For all projects coming through the EPMO, they too need robust business cases.
Head of EPMO (Awit)	I can understand putting projects that we haven't started on hold, but why pause in-flight projects? This is going to make people concerned. Who's going to determine which projects are non-essential?
Head of P&C (Swaty)	I agree with Awit. Also, making it hard to backfill will send the wrong message to the team. It will make my team look incompetent. Why don't we just tell our line managers exactly what's going on and that we need to address some of these measures?
Head of finance (Chien)	No, we cannot tell people. Ken was clear about this.
	From the project perspective, give me the list of in-flight projects, and I'll determine which ones are non-essential.

Awit looks nervous about this, as Chien is not a key stakeholder and does not know what is deemed important.

Head of P&C (Swaty)	Our teams have a certain level of autonomy and can go to external recruitment as well. What do you want to do about this?
Head of finance (Chien)	Swaty, you need to change the process and have all hiring requests come through you before external recruitment is engaged. We cannot have things slipping through the cracks.

Head of P&C (Swaty)	This is going to cause issues and is going to freak people out.
	We've hired some pretty mature senior leaders. I'm sure they can handle this. Keeping people in the dark is going to cause us problems and impact our culture.
Head of finance (Chien)	Ken is relying on the two of you to manage this, and that includes the cultural and morale aspects.

Six months later, when projects have unfolded.

Narrator	The business deliverables have been impacted. Staff retention statistics are showing a dramatic increase. Team morale across all departments is impacted and projects that were put on hold are now considered urgent as they have not been revisited until the original instruction to hold was put in place.
CEO (Ken)	Chien, we're having really big problems with the team's morale.
Head of finance (Chien)	I can see this, but we've managed to keep our costs controlled – in fact they're looking really good.
CEO (Ken)	But we haven't delivered some of our important projects that will improve market share. What's going on?
Head of finance (Chien)	I instructed P&C to not backfill and to not hire any new staff, as instructed. I also instructed the EPMO to hold any new projects and to pause in-flight projects that I felt were non-essential.
CEO (Ken)	Those were not my instructions, Chien.
	I specifically asked to just go slow on the backfills, but we still need to do this. New hires we needed to stop, but not the backfills.
	As for the projects, I said clearly to only pause projects that had not started. I said nothing about pausing in-flight projects; and, on that note, who determined which projects to hold?
Head of finance (Chien)	I advised the EPMO which projects to put on hold.
CEO (Ken)	How would you know what was important and what was not?
Head of finance (Chien)	I made an educated guess, Ken. I did as I was asked, and I've saved money for this organization.

CFO (Lakshmi)	Yes, you did do this, Chien. But, as we weren't backfilling roles, team members started speculating on the business's prospects for the future. And, as we had paused all in-flight projects, this also sent the wrong message.
	Our staff retention is declining and we're not backfilling. And now, even though we've saved money, we're in a worse position than before.
	Ken, we really should have brought more people into the loop on these activities. This is really damaging our corporate brand now.
CEO (Ken)	Yes, yes, you're right, Lakshmi.
	Chien, I appreciate the work you've done, but we need to unwind some of this and try to repair the damage.
Narrator	In the subsequent days, Ken brings his leaders into discussions to go over the original plan and where they find themselves – seeking help from his leaders now, when he should have done this at the beginning of the process.

10×Generation

In the 10×Generation state, issues felt at the strategic tier are visible at the tactical and operational tiers.

All teams work together to resolve problems and work towards common goals. Rumours are non-existent, as conversations and decisions are visible to all. Discussions are curated to suit the level of audience; however, the same overarching message is clearly discussed.

All team members are invited to add input in their areas of expertise, and all options are considered. If an option is not appropriate, the person or team that put it forward is thanked for their input and given feedback as to why their idea was not adopted.

All team members feel a part of the whole. As an organization grows, it gets harder to ensure that all team members are in the loop regarding decisions. This is where the 10×Generation principles will assist regardless of the size of the organization.

This ensures that, at each tier and in each department, there is a strategy that links in with the overall business strategy, and that these documents live and breathe with the organization as it grows and changes.

We have seen what happens when leaders do not trust their teams, and how detrimental this is to productivity and retention. Let's see what happens when departments focus solely on their own deliverables and forget that the organization, like an organism, thrives on trust and togetherness.

Act 2, Scene 8: The paradox of departmental success – breaking down the walls

#Startup #Scaleup #SMB #Enterprise #LargeEnterprise

#Tactical #Strategic

In an SMB organization, the biggest challenges between departments can vary depending on the nature of the business and the specific departments involved. However, the most common issue is departments operating independently and prioritizing their own goals over the success of the company as a whole.

Each department may view itself as the most important, and may compete with other departments for recognition. The by-product of this is a failure to share information, which leads to duplication of effort, inefficiencies, and missed opportunities for innovation or improvement.

The scene opens with several employees at a large corporate office, all sitting in their cubicles, typing away on their computers. In the background, we hear the sounds of phones ringing, printers whirring and people chattering.

Cut to a meeting room, where several executives are seated around a large table. They are discussing the company's performance metrics. Lakshmi, the CFO, is leading the meeting.

CFO (Lakshmi)	All right, let's dive into the numbers. Sales are up 5% from the last quarter, which is great news for the company.
Head of sales and marketing (Hans)	That's fantastic, Lakshmi. Our marketing campaigns really paid off this quarter.
CFO (Lakshmi)	Yes, and we're also seeing a 2% increase in customer satisfaction scores. Great job, Kelly.

Krish, the head of customer service, nods appreciatively.

CFO (Lakshmi)	But let's not forget that we missed our productivity targets this quarter. We need to work on improving efficiency.
Head of IT ops (Oleg)	Hold on a second, Lakshmi. We hit our production targets, but we had some unexpected downtime due to equipment failures.
CFO (Lakshmi)	I understand that, Oleg, but we need to focus on overall productivity. We can't have any missed opportunities.

Narrator	As the meeting continues, it becomes clear that each department is solely focused on its individual metrics. There's no collaboration between departments and no focus on the company's bottom line.

Cut to the cubicles, where an employee looks frustrated as they try to work on a project. They need input from another department, but that department is too focused on its own metrics to help.

Cut back to the meeting room, where Lakshmi is wrapping up the meeting.

CFO (Lakshmi)	All right, great meeting, everyone. Keep up the good work, and let's hit those targets next quarter.

As the meeting ends, we zoom in on Lakshmi's face. We see a look of concern as she realizes that the siloed culture in the organization is leading to missed opportunities for innovation and improvement.

CFO (Lakshmi)	*(To herself)* I can't believe that focusing solely on individual department metrics can actually harm the company's bottom line. We need to find a way to encourage collaboration and break down these silos.

The scene ends with Lakshmi looking thoughtful as the curtain drops.

10×Generation

The dark side of departmental metrics creates a competitive and adversarial culture. It also discourages innovation and risk-taking, and sometimes can lead to unethical behaviours.

Leaders need to strike the right balance between individual and team metrics, and to create a culture that values both individual and collective success.

One of the most practical ways of achieving these aims is to encourage events that promote cross-functional teams: leaders can create teams that bring together employees from different departments to work on specific projects. This not only encourages collaboration, but also helps employees gain a better understanding of how their work impacts other areas of the company.

We most commonly see this behaviour in a 'hack-a-thon' or a 'strat-a-thon' (for strategic initiatives), where, instead of rewarding individual departments, leaders offer incentives based on cross-team success. This encourages teams to work together towards common goals and fosters a sense of collective responsibility for the success of the company.

10×Generation suggests the motto of leadership as:

'One company, one goal: Aligning individual and team metrics for maximum impact.'

As each issue is teased out, it is clear that no matter what size your organization is, it can still be impacted by these scenarios. The next section looks at the enterprise-sized organization.

Enterprise

With an increase in size and complexity, we see a dramatic increase in departmental size and structure. In the enterprise, the tactical view is much larger than the operational view. With added complexity comes greater size, and with greater size come more processes. With additional processes, more human capital is needed to continue to run the organization.

> *Companies, as they grow to become multi-billion-dollar entities, somehow lose their vision. They insert lots of layers of middle management between the people running the company and the people doing the work. They no longer have an inherent feel or a passion about the products. The creative people, who are the ones who care passionately, have to persuade five layers of management to do what they know is the right thing to do.*
>
> Steve Jobs[38]

When the right thing to do is lost and silos are created, we see what happens in our next scene.

Act 2, Scene 9: Too many cooks in the corporate kitchen – surviving the corporate jungle

#Scaleup #SMB #Enterprise #LargeEnterprise

#Operational #Tactical #Strategic

When companies grow large and have many departments, each department cares only about its own roadmap, creating dissent across teams. Unlike in our previous scene, we see a team member desperately wanting to help others but being hamstrung by politics.

Narrator   Despite having a large pool of talented teams and a solid product roadmap, the company has a lot of redundancy among projects and a shortage of resources for key projects.

The stage is set in a cosy suburban home office, with a large window that lets in plenty of natural light. A desk is positioned in the centre of the room, surrounded by shelves filled with books and knick-knacks. A comfortable chair sits in front of the desk, and a computer and other office equipment are neatly arranged on the surface. Li, the UX/UI (user experience/interface) designer, is logging on to the Zoom call that has been scheduled for 10:00am.

Senior PM (Jackson)	Good morning, everyone. Can you hear me OK?
Team members	Good morning! Yes, we can hear you loud and clear.
Senior PM (Jackson)	Great, let's get started. So, Awit, what's on the agenda for today's call?
Head of EPMO (Awit)	*(Speaking on mute)*
Senior PM (Jackson)	You're on mute, Awit.
Head of EPMO (Awit)	*(Fumbling to un-mute herself)* Oh, apologies, I think I do this at least once a day. We have a few items to discuss, but the main one is the status of the project. Li, can you give us an update on where we're at?
UX/UI designer (Li)	Sure, I can give an update. We're currently on track with our development schedule and have made good progress on the features we planned for this sprint. However, I was approached by Mark from the FinOps team, who wanted me to test a quick UX journey and A/B test it.
Senior PM (Jackson)	That doesn't belong on our roadmap, and we don't have the resources or manpower to take on any more work. They're planning to hire a new UX designer soon, they can offload that then.
UX/UI designer (Li)	But … I have the capacity, and it's my job to help with UX journeys. Without my support, the FinOps team will miss their deliverables.
Senior PM (Jackson)	Li, you know how important our roadmap is. We can't afford to have you wasting your time on their deliverables. Just focus on our work, OK?
UX/UI designer (Li)	We're supposed to be a team and help each other. I have the bandwidth, Jackson. Awit, you're head of EPMO – what do you think?

Head of EPMO (Awit)	I agree with Jackson. He has a job to do to deliver his roadmap. If the other teams want time prioritized, then they need to request it, just like everyone else. We'll then go through the prioritization process and assign team members to this.
UX/UI designer (Li)	But by the time they go through that process, their deliverables will well and truly be late.
Head of EPMO (Awit)	That's not your concern, Li. Just focus on your work and your deliverables. Jackson, let's move on, please.
Narrator	Li decides to help the team anyway and enables it to meet its deliverables.

Knowing that the time spent means that multiple projects can be achieved is much better for business outcomes. |

10×Generation

In the 10×Generation state, relevant processes can be implemented, but with a view of remaining lean. Over-burdensome processes cause teams and individuals to work around them. When this happens, all teams lose visibility as to what is happening in the organization.

It is important to avoid having silos among departments, and to encourage communication and collaboration. This can involve creating opportunities for employees from different departments to work together on projects, in a 'team of teams' setting, hosting regular meetings where staff from various departments can share updates and ideas.

Another effective strategy is to implement systems and processes that facilitate cross-departmental collaboration, such as shared OKRs and work ceremonies. It's also important for leadership to prioritize collaboration and break down departmental barriers, so that employees feel supported and empowered to work together.

According to Gartner, working collaboratively means that parts of the culture need to change. Defining how to measure collaboration to drive behaviour change is key to a successful transition.[39] Cultural change is the hardest type of change to achieve in any size of organization, but doubly so in an enterprise. Unlike in the collaboration scenario above, we have different issues when a department wants to own its own destiny but not manage it end to end. It cannot have it both ways – but let's see what happens when it asks exactly for that.

Act 2, Scene 10: Hold up, that's not my job

#SMB #Enterprise #LargeEnterprise

#Tactical #Strategic

In the marketing department, there is contention as to whether the technology function should be involved in the marketing technology decisions. The MarTech team believes that it is separate when it comes to the decision-making, but leans heavily on the technology department when there is a need to troubleshoot problems, keep the lights on and manage the vendor relationships.

Lights come up and we are presented with three people in a meeting room. The discussion is becoming heated between the parties.

Narrator	When two departments cannot find an amicable way of working together, we start to see friction points across a business. The larger the business becomes, the more friction points we see.
	Here we have a prime example of two departments with similar underpinning needs that have not been able to work together.
Head of sales and marketing (Hans)	Morrison, what's happening with the MarTech stack? We haven't been able to use some of our key applications in days. What are you doing?
MarTech lead (Morrison)	I have raised this with technology, and as usual they're dragging their heels on this one. MarTech just isn't important enough to be looked at with urgency, I guess.
Head of technology (Mike)	*(Getting frustrated)* Morrison, that isn't the case at all. Technology has very little visibility into the MarTech stack. Decisions are made outside of technology, and then when there's an issue you expect that my team will be able to support you.
MarTech lead (Morrison)	That is just an excuse. Your team manage the infrastructure and have to be held accountable for what's on it.
Head of technology (Mike)	We can ensure that servers are available and that infrastructure is stable, but we can't be held responsible for the applications that are in use.
	As an example: if a server needs to be patched, we need to do this but we can't be held responsible if the MarTech application doesn't work with the upgrade. That has to sit within the marketing team.

MarTech lead (Morrison)	We can't manage with that as well as provide the application support to the team. We're not set up for this.
	You just need to do your job. You're IT. You should be acting like it.
Head of technology (Mike)	Morrison, if you don't adequately hand over application support and loop IT into the technology decisions being made, then IT can't help you. We're happy to give you a server and ensure its reliability, but the buck stops there.
Head of sales and marketing (Hans)	This is ridiculous. My sales and marketing team are hamstrung. We need to get the next campaign delivered, and we can't do this.
Head of technology (Mike)	I'm sorry, Hans, but I don't have anyone in my team that understands any of your applications – we don't have any relationships with your vendors.
	All I can suggest is that Morrison contacts the vendors and works with them on fixing the problems, but we can't help.
Head of sales and marketing (Hans)	Thanks, Mike.
	Morrison, you'd best get on to the vendors and try to fix this issue.
Narrator	In many large organizations we see disparate teams splintering off from the main technology function in an effort to deliver solutions faster than the perceived speed of IT.
	MarTech uses specialized applications for the work it does, but in the end the need for support remains the same.
	We see directly what happens when there is a disconnect between who is responsible and who is accountable for the technical stack.

Two weeks later, the MarTech issues are ongoing with no resolution in sight.

Head of sales and marketing (Hans)	Mike, we're in a real pickle. The team can't do their work, and my team have been unable to get any traction with the vendor. I need some help from you and your team.
Head of technology (Mike)	Hans, we can look into it, but we need to find a way of working better together so that this doesn't continue to happen.
Head of sales and marketing (Hans)	Absolutely. Once we get this latest campaign out the door, let's regroup and sort this out.

Lights dim and the scene ends.

10×Generation

In the 10×Generation state, there is visibility horizontally and vertically in an organization between operational, tactical and strategic tiers. In the tactical tier, we have individual departments that may want to embark on their own solutions. This is encouraged in the 10×Generation state; however, ensuring that all other impacted departments are included well before decisions are made will provide the visibility and support that is needed. This will avoid the issues seen in this scenario.

This example is different from shadow IT, as the MarTech team has engaged IT, but not in a way that enables cross-functional operations. The impacts of the problems have crippled a department and impacted delivery. This has a flow-on effect on the entire organization. When one department embarks on decisions that are formed in isolation, this will always have flow-on effects that are not understood at the start of the process.

With clearly defined roles and responsibilities, the issues experienced in this scenario are minimized and removed, enabling all departments to work efficiently, knowing which department and which roles are accountable and responsible for each function.

Working with each other, sharing knowledge and utilizing each other's strengths builds stronger relationships and provides more robust, reliable solutions for all departments. The removal of assumptions about clearly defined ways of working, plus broad consensus, leads to agreed actions and responsibilities, which moves the organization closer to the 10×Generation state.

As the organization opens up clear lines of communication, it creates consistency across departments and creates a virtuous cycle that each department can get behind. Let's see how the 10×Generation state can help bring order to disorder in our next scene.

Act 2 Scene 11: From chaos to consistency across the enterprise

#Enterprise #LargeEnterprise

#Tactical #Strategic

Enterprise organizations can be complex, with multiple departments, business units and subsidiaries operating across different geographies, markets and regulatory environments. This can create challenges in terms of coordination, integration, and alignment and understanding of local needs and culture.

This leads to departments having limited agility, and so they may struggle to respond quickly and effectively to changes in the market or competitive landscape. This can be due to bureaucratic processes, a lack of flexibility, or a focus on short-term results and worse, short-term thinking.

The scene opens with a projected view of the vast campus of a technology giant; the hustle and bustle of employees walking, talking and working on their laptops can be seen in the background.

Cut to boardroom. A group of executives sit around a large conference table, flipping through thick stacks of papers and reports. They all look frustrated and stressed.

COO (Shane)	I can't believe we're still dealing with these inconsistent processes across our different business units. It's costing us more time and even more money!
CIO (Ajay)	And don't get me started on the bureaucratic processes. It takes forever to get anything done around here.
CEO (Ken)	Plus, the focus on short-term results is killing our ability to innovate and adapt to the market.

Cut to P&C department. An employee sits in front of a computer, filling out countless forms and applications. She looks tired and annoyed.

| Office admin (Liya) | *(Muttering to herself)* Why do I have to fill out so many forms just to transfer to a different department? And why does it take so long for the people and culture team to process anything? |

Cut to marketing department. A group of employees huddle around a whiteboard, brainstorming ideas for a new marketing campaign. Hans looks sceptical.

| Head of sales and marketing (Hans) | I don't think this idea will work. It's too risky. |
| Head of product (Roberto) | Who cares? As long as we hit our numbers for this quarter, that's all that matters. |

Cut to technology department. A team of engineers sit in front of their computers, trying to fix a glitch in the system. They look frustrated and stressed.

| IT ops engineer (Joey) | This glitch is going to take forever to fix. And we don't even have the resources we need to do it. |
| Principal engineer (Dagmar) | I know. But we have to make do with what we have. Management doesn't want to allocate any more resources to this project. |

Cut to CEO's office. The CEO sits behind her desk, staring at the reports on the screen with the CFO. She looks stressed and overwhelmed.

CFO (Lakshmi)	We need to do something about all these problems. We're too big and too bureaucratic to be flexible and innovative. We're going to lose our edge if we don't change things soon.

10×Generation

There is no silver bullet for overcoming fragmented data and inconsistent processes in the enterprise world. There are, though, many frameworks that help with strategies to unify the enterprise:

- **Lean Six Sigma**[40] A framework that is focused on process improvement and aims to reduce waste and variability in processes. It uses data and analytics to identify areas for improvement and implement standardized processes across the organization
- **ISO 9001**[41] A quality management system that provides a framework for implementing consistent processes and procedures across an organization. It is designed to ensure that products and services meet customer and regulatory requirements
- **ITIL**[42] A framework for IT service management that provides a standardized set of processes and procedures for managing IT services. It is designed to improve efficiency and effectiveness in IT operations
- **COBIT (Control Objectives for Information and Related Technology)**[43] A framework for IT governance that provides a set of guidelines for managing IT processes and resources. It is designed to ensure that IT supports the organization's goals and objectives
- **TOGAF (The Open Group Architecture Framework)**[44] A framework for enterprise architecture that provides a standardized set of processes and procedures for managing the development and implementation of IT systems. It is designed to improve alignment between IT and business goals.

By using one or more of these frameworks, an enterprise can implement standardized processes and procedures across jurisdictions. This can help to reduce variability, improve efficiency, and promote a culture of collaboration and consistency across the organization.

The 10×Generation state looks at existing models and frameworks that enable an organization to reach consistency. What it doesn't encourage is layering many frameworks and creating even more bureaucracy. The use of frameworks should be considered as a way of reducing noise, improving consistency, and taking what works best for your organization without weighing it down with undue processes.

In an effort to reach consistency, every organization needs to look towards a different way of structuring itself. The old ways of working are no longer able to help organizations achieve the growth potential they strive for. Let's throw the 10×Generation spanner into the works as we look at the next scene and posit the question: 'Why are we afraid of cross-functional teams?'

Act 2, Scene 12: Resistance to cross-functional teams – the team of teams revolution

#Startup #Scaleup #SMB #Enterprise #LargeEnterprise

#Tactical #Strategic

Why do enterprise organizations have a resistance to cross-functional teams? Could *team of teams* be the answer?

Large companies often have established processes, systems and hierarchies that make it difficult to implement cross-functional teams. These processes, systems and hierarchies may be deeply ingrained in the company's culture, making it hard to change. Resistance to change is also a natural human response, and large companies are no exception. Cross-functional teams require a shift in mindset, and most leaders are resistant to this.

Is it possible to break these hierarchies, the old-school mindset, the lack of trust and the fear of change?

The scene opens at the headquarters of a large enterprise organization. A group of executives sit around a conference table. They all look stern and serious.

Head of P&C (Swaty)	I don't think we should have cross-functional teams. We need to keep our departments separate and focus on our specific objectives.
Head of product (Roberto)	I agree. Cross-functional teams will only create confusion and slow us down.
Head of architecture (Cillian)	But we're missing out on the benefits of collaboration and innovation that cross-functional teams can bring.

Cut to the adjacent room, where the marketing team is having a meeting. A group of marketers sit around a table, brainstorming ideas for a new product launch. Hans, the head of sales and marketing, looks frustrated.

Head of sales and marketing (Hans)	I wish we could work with the technology department on this. They could help us create something really innovative. Or at least tell us if our ideas are remotely possible.
Junior marketer (Geraldine)	Don't even bother. The technology department has their own priorities, and they're not going to work with us on this.

Cut to the technology floor, where cross-functional technology teams sit. ('Cross-functional' implies product, developers and quality assurance.)

A group of engineers sit in front of their computers, working on a new software project.

MarTech engineer (Sally)	I wish we could get input from the marketing department on this. They could help us make sure we're creating something customers actually want.
Principal engineer (Dagmar)	Don't count on it. The marketing department doesn't understand what we do, and they'll just get in the way.
Narrator	This is a common scenario across different departments in an organization: people and culture, finance, legal, product, technology and many more.
	Departments create additional processes in an effort to reduce miscommunication; however, the outcome is greater inefficiencies. The cost is not just to collaboration and economies of scale. The bigger cost and lost opportunity are to innovation and agility!

10×Generation

The idea of multiple teams that collaborate and work together towards a common goal or objective is known to all senior leaders. Yet large organizations often implement a hierarchy that makes it difficult to support this structure.

Most organizations require collaboration and coordination across multiple teams to achieve complex goals that are beyond the capabilities of a single team. 'Team of teams', a concept first described in *Team of Teams: New rules of engagement for a complex world* by General Stanley McChrystal,[45] describes the approach that the US military in Iraq and Afghanistan used to address the challenges of fighting a decentralized and agile enemy. Since then, the concept has been used successfully in a variety of industries, including the military, healthcare and software development.

A team of teams structure should and must be used in large, complex organizations or in situations where teams need to work together in a dynamic, fast-paced environment. In this approach, each team or individual is responsible for a specific area of work, but is also part of a larger team that includes other teams and individuals working towards the same objective.

Imagine a world where a team of teams has members from every department and can be scaled, saving huge sums on resourcing.

The team of teams has a flavour that most technology organizations are aware of – where the company organizes its development teams into *squads*, which are small, cross-functional teams, each responsible for a specific area of the product. These squads are then organized into larger *tribes*, which are collections of squads working towards a common goal. The tribes are then part of a *chapter*, a group of people with similar skills who can share knowledge and best practices across tribes.

What's missing are other departments to form the larger team of teams – a decentralized management structure where teams are organized around specific projects rather than functional areas.

The best example of this has been in the healthcare world where, to improve patient outcomes and reduce costs, the Cleveland Clinic implemented a team of teams approach to improve the care of patients with heart failure. The hospital organized multidisciplinary teams of physicians, nurses and other healthcare professionals to work together and share information to improve patient care.

The 10×Generation state leans on ideas from the team of teams structure by providing the guiding principles to embed a collaborative focus and ensure large organizations are able to embrace collaboration at the core.

All of the scenarios in Act 2 have further demonstrated the issues that the operational tier will experience in an organization of any size. In the final act, we will focus on the strategic tier. Some think this is the most important tier, as this is where leadership decisions stem from – but in the 10×Generation state, decisions are made throughout, not pushed from top to bottom.

In contrast with the 'top-down versus bottom-up' approach to management, the 10×Generation believes in the 'cyclical' approach, as shown in Figure 19.

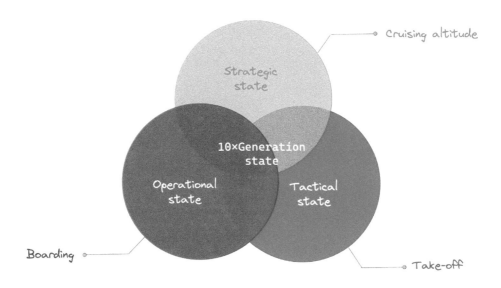

Figure 19 10×Generation 'cyclical' approach

Act 3: The echoes of isolation and innovation

In Act 3 we look into the issues being faced at a strategic or executive level in an organization, which in the 10×Generation state is known as the *strategic view* (see Figure 20). In this tier we will examine each of the main challenges as seen from the executive view. When an organization grows and starts putting in the strategic layer, this is where an understanding of the lower two tiers is often missed, and visibility becomes muddied. What is important in the lower tiers is seen as less important at the strategic view, when in actual fact it is vitally important.

Figure 20 Radius of growth: The strategic layer

The difference between the strategic view and the others is that when an organization is struggling, the strategic executive will make decisions from a place of miscommunication and unknowing, and this will inevitably lead to a decision to act based on assumption and poor advice. Reduction in headcount, digital transformation, poor hiring decisions and the like will become by-products of an ill-informed strategic tier.

The impact of underperformance or missed targets is felt in the strategic view, and will have the most profound impact on the organization if the decisions are made in haste and through a narrow lens.

Setting the strategic scene

In this third act, we see the interaction between all three tiers and the characters within them. As in the previous acts, we will be revisiting each organizational type: startup or scaleup, SMB and enterprise. As before, each scenario is a vignette that builds on the key challenges that an organization will encounter, but from the view of the executive.

Startup or scaleup

For startups or scaleups, we provide scenarios that are shown at the founder or CEO level. Generally, in a startup or scaleup, the burgeoning executive is slowly being articulated and grown in an immature organization. As the leaders are learning their craft at the executive level, there will be pitfalls that will be fleshed out further in the coming scenes.

In the first scene, we see what happens when decisions are made with a limited understanding of the impacts at a team level.

Act 3, Scene 1: When less is less

#Startup #Scaleup #Enterprise #LargeEnterprise

#Tactical #Strategic

As a result of the recent end-of-financial-year announcement stating that the company's objectives had not been met, the senior leadership has decided to cut down on hiring costs. The product and technology teams are not sure why their area of the organization is the only one being targeted. There is a hiring freeze, which will impact the ability of the product and technology teams to deliver on an already over-committed roadmap.

The scene is set in the office kitchen, with the CIO, Ajay, adding another shot to his third cup of coffee of the day, after the meetings where he was told to cut costs and freeze hiring.

All new hiring requests will need to be approved by the CFO in future. The heads of product and technology have just walked in, and overhear the boss mumbling to himself.

Narrator	There have been many meetings in the past to discuss product and technology investments and the accumulating technical debt.
	The technology teams were tasked with creating a risk register and a wiki page that highlights all new initiatives and the accumulated technical debt.
	The product teams were tasked with ensuring everything on the roadmap was scrutinized by senior leadership.
	There were clearly a few 'big rocks' that could save the company huge sums of money but were never actioned.
Head of technology (Mike)	Hey Ajay, more coffee?
CIO (Ajay)	I'm having a 'déjà brew', just like the meeting I'm coming out of where they want to freeze hiring while we have more projects to work on.
Head of technology (Mike)	Why does this not surprise me? It's like déjà vu from every technology company I've worked at.

The 'heads of' and Ajay cancel their next meeting and head to the local pub to have a chat on what this change means.

In the 1940s-style classic pub, Ajay is sitting at the back of a U-shaped booth. He is having a sip of his favourite beer and reacting to the cost cuts, while both Jackson and Roberto are shaking their heads in despair.

CIO (Ajay)	The CFO thinks we're not utilizing our budget well; also we haven't performed very well as an organization. The overall revenue figures aren't looking good! So he's convinced our CEO to freeze all hiring till we're back on track.
Head of product (Roberto)	Does that mean that everything new on my roadmap is also going to pause?
Head of technology (Mike)	You are kidding, aren't you?
CIO (Ajay)	Mike's right: we need to deliver a few more strategic initiatives with the same headcount.
Head of technology (Mike)	Why haven't you educated them on looking at some low-hanging fruit? We could save a ton of money on the tech debt items we have, by culling some of the duplication in vendors, and reignite some of our cloud automation initiatives.

CIO (Ajay)	You know they don't understand technology – our CFO for the fifth time this year asked me, 'What do you mean by "tech debt", Ajay?'

10×Generation

In today's agile ways of working, one of the key ingredients to being truly agile is missed.

Most non-technical senior leaders struggle to understand technology and treat it as a black box. They speak with the CTO or CIO when necessary, yet wonder why technology appears to be a black hole of misunderstood costs.

> Lines of Code! = Quality of Code

We see in popular media the idea that the number of lines of code is equal to throughput; just because a program has a lot of code, that does not mean it is well written or efficient. Good code should be easy to read and understand, with clear and concise logic that achieves the desired functionality.

It's the job of the CIO and/or CTO to educate senior leadership, creating a balance between tech-speak and business language. It is also their job to empower leaders in the technology teams – all the way from senior engineers to principals and directors – to do the same.

Education has to start from a grass-roots level and be supported from the top down. It will then permeate all the way through the organization. Every stakeholder needs to understand the ways of working – how a product is conceived from inception to production to post-production.

Technology leaders and teams need to stop falling into the trap of having to build pet projects or platform projects to influence senior leaders. Instead, everything that is built should be aligned with a business outcome and shared, as would be the case with a new product.

Make how to deliver software efficiencies a part of every conversation you have with your stakeholders, no matter which layer they are in. Consider everyone to be a stakeholder.

Gartner says: 'CIOs either need to recover from the past or prevent future underinvestment, as new cost liabilities are continually added to the technology portfolio. Report cost liabilities to identify your technology debt position, then develop business plans that create net wealth, not just debt.'[46]

Eventually, technical debt needs to be repaid, and having open and honest conversations about it enables action plans to be added as part of the product roadmap. When decisions are under review, there will come a time when an organization looks at whether it should build or buy software. We see this play out in our next scenario.

Act 3, Scene 2: The art of decision-making – build vs buy

#Startup #Scaleup #SMB #Enterprise #LargeEnterprise

#Operational #Tactical #Strategic

The conundrum that many leaders face, whether they work in IT or in any other department, is whether they should invest in building their own solutions or look at commercial off-the-shelf (COTS) software.

Narrator	The technology leadership team requires a decision from the senior leadership team on a tough problem: should the organization build a software solution in-house, or should it buy one from an outside vendor?

The stage is set in a bustling city, in a meeting room with skyscrapers towering in the background. The CTO is bringing in a whiteboard and markers. A group of product and technology people are huddled together around the whiteboard.

CTO (Jane)	This is it, everyone. This is where we'll decide on how we build this project. Let's share our opinions and get started.
Principal engineer (Dagmar)	One advantage of building the software ourselves is that we can tailor it to our exact needs and specifications. We won't have to compromise on any features, and we'll know exactly how the software works under the hood.
CPO (Alec)	That's true, but building software from scratch can be a time-consuming and expensive process. It might be more cost effective to buy a solution that's already been developed and tested by someone else.
CFO (Lakshmi)	That's a good point. Buying software also has the added benefit of being a one-time cost, whereas building software will require ongoing investment in terms of resources and personnel.
CTO (Jane)	On the other hand, buying software means we're at the mercy of the vendor. If they go out of business or stop supporting the software, we could be left in a difficult situation. With in-house software, we have complete control and can make any necessary updates or changes as needed.

10×Generation

In the end, the decision to build or buy software will depend on many factors. The golden rule is: 'Never build something that isn't your business.'

A good example is to never build a bespoke authentication system unless you are in the business of providing authentication services. Always ask the question: will the software be a part of your business's core offering?

The most important metric is 'time to value', which should have a direct impact on return on investment (ROI). Aggressive growth goals might require a different strategy, where it might be worthwhile to buy technology or acquire an entire company outright.

Always take advantage of economies of scale, as the benefits of your software should compound over time!

Forrester summarizes this well: 'In the digital era, software is an expression of the business. Firms can't buy this; they must create it using a blend of customization and composition.'[47]

Once an organization has mastered the build versus buy scenario, it will ultimately be faced with the dilemma of engaging consultants. For many working in the consulting space, having an inexperienced customer can lead to an extended consulting opportunity, where you can help an organization to realize its goals. The issue faced by both consultants and organizations alike is when the scope of the engagement is unclear. When this happens, no one wins.

Act 3, Scene 3: When is a consultant not a consultant?

#Startup #Scaleup #SMB #Enterprise #LargeEnterprise

#Operational #Tactical #Strategic

In this scenario we see an inexperienced founder working in a startup. The company needs a strategic vision and the right senior leaders to bring this to life, but the founder is uncertain about who should be brought in. He is the ideas man, and this leadership stuff is challenging and not something he is comfortable with.

He is being advised to bring in expensive consultants to flesh out a leadership team and to work with the business, instead of focusing on bringing in the right long-term talent to support the business. Consultants should not be brought in to do the work for an ongoing function. Let's see what happens when they are engaged.

We see an office, cluttered with papers on the desk, a laptop with dual monitors and an executive working behind the desk. The executive (our founder) is staring intently at the monitors, fixated on the task he is working on.

Narrator	The stage is set with our young founder, Scott, who is focused on spreadsheets, confirming the weekly P&L of the business. It seems only months ago that his idea took flight, and now he is acting as CEO in a rapidly growing, soon to be scaleup, business.
	Having never run a business in the past, Scott sees gaps in the leadership team that are becoming a problem. The best piece of advice from the founder's mentor was to focus on cash flow and the P&L, and the founder is doing just that.

In walks the mentor (Jim).

Mentor (Jim)	It seems to me that you've been staring at that spreadsheet for hours. Anything I can help with?
Founder (Scott)	I have a good handle on the numbers, but I'm concerned about some of the major gaps I have in my leadership team. I have a heavy-hitting CTO and CPO. I know we need more people, and I think I need to bring in an HR guru, and I need to invest in a CFO. I think the time is right.
Mentor (Jim)	Those senior leadership roles are going to cost you quite a bit. Perhaps you need to consider alternatives. Remember cash flow is king, and you don't want to be paying out large salaries as you're scaling the business.
Founder (Scott)	What are you thinking?
Mentor (Jim)	Why not bring in some consultants? I know a few people who might be just what you need. It may cost a little bit more, but it'll be for a short term. Bring them in, have them set things up and then hire who you need.
Founder (Scott)	If you think that's the best option, I'll give it a go.
Narrator	Our founder interviews quite a few consultants and chooses two people to step in and support the business, but things do not go to plan.
	The first consultant has come out of a large organization and is used to managing large teams. Unfortunately, they are not able to set up teams from scratch, and after three months it becomes apparent that the consultant just isn't working out.
	The second consultant is not suited to working in a scaleup organization, and expected to have many more team members to do the lion's share of the work. The founder has had to step in multiple times to assist, and this has impacted on his ability to focus on other areas of the business.

10×Generation

Consultants have a place, and can often offer a different viewpoint for a startup or organization that is growing rapidly. However, there will be situations where consultants will not fulfil a need and should be considered more cautiously. When thinking about bringing in consultants, it is vital to have a clear line of sight as to the outcomes you are expecting.

In the 10×Generation state, here are some things to consider:

- If the organization lacks the level of maturity to understand the type of consultants needed to meet the gap, the added expense may be prohibitive. Take the time to do the research into what you are wanting to achieve. Interview a few consulting companies and see whether they offer what you want

- If the organization has a healthy culture that will be impacted negatively by installing consultants, this should be a red flag to the leaders in the organization. Destabilizing a startup or scaleup could make the difference between successfully clearing the next hurdle and shutting up shop

- If the organization is unable to define its own strategy clearly, the scope and objectives of the consultancy's work may be difficult to quantify, which will impact the consultant's ability to deliver. Sometimes bringing in a strategic consultant to help create a strategy is the first step. With this in place it's easier to recruit top talent, as you have a clearly defined and articulated strategy that others can implement and follow.

In general, bringing in consultants to meet a need at the strategic level should be carefully considered. Understanding the strategy, and communicating it across all tiers in the organization, will ensure clarity of purpose for all team members. Then, if additional headcount is needed, this can be approached with a clear indication of what type of resource to bring in.

With an open and transparent process, it may be that full-time team members with the best skill and cultural fit would be a better option than consultants who have less buy-in to the organization's strategic vision. Bringing in more team members to fill in the gaps means that the complexities of wearing multiple hats may be addressed; this can be seen in the next scenario.

Act 3, Scene 4: Complexities of wearing multiple hats

#Startup #Scaleup #SMB

#Tactical #Strategic

Wearing multiple hats as part of the senior leadership in a startup or scaleup can be both exciting and challenging. On one hand, it allows leaders to be involved in many different aspects of the business and to have a broader perspective of the company. On the other hand, it can also lead to a number of complexities and challenges.

The scene opens at the sleek and modern office building. A group of executives, all in their mid-30s to early 40s and dressed in business-casual attire, are gathered around a large conference table. The room is modern and minimalist, with large windows providing a view of the city skyline.

We see the executives as they begin reviewing documents for the meeting. One of them is on the phone with a potential investor, another is reviewing marketing materials, and another is working on financial projections while waiting for the meeting to commence.

CEO (Ken)	*(To the group)* So, we need to start thinking about our next funding round. We're going to need to show some serious growth if we want to attract investors.

The other executives nod in agreement.

Head of product (Roberto)	What about our user acquisition strategy? We've been seeing good numbers, but I think we can do better.
CEO (Ken)	Yes, we need to double down on that. What's our customer acquisition cost looking like these days?
CFO (Lakshmi)	It's still high, but we're working on optimizing our ad spend to bring it down.

Suddenly, the door bursts open, and a young employee rushes in, looking panicked.

Young employee (Glenn)	We have a problem with our app and the website. They're down!
CEO (Ken)	OK, let's get on it. Have you contacted the development team? Why do we keep encountering these problems?
Head of product (Roberto)	Yes, I see on Slack that the dev team is on it. I think it's our authentication system – we should build a bespoke system soon.
CEO (Ken)	All right, add that to your roadmap ASAP. Can someone else take over the funding strategy discussion for now?

Another executive nods and takes over the discussion while the CEO rushes out of the room.

It is a common scenario at a startup where the leaders have to wear multiple hats. In the above scene, we don't have anyone from technology in the room, and yet product has decided to add a bespoke authentication system to its roadmap.

Not only is building a bespoke authentication system a complex process – it also has maintenance and scalability challenges that only a small cohort can understand.

Fast forward five years. The business has reached SMB size and wants to replace the authentication system. Instead of the bespoke solution in place, it wants to use something tried and tested in the market, a system that other organizations use. If this had been addressed when the organization was smaller, it would have enabled security, scalability, compliance and integration with other vendors, and it would have been for *free*!

To do this now, not only is it a major people and business cost, but also the entire system will need to be re-architected.

10×Generation

In the startup phase, executives have no other option but to have their senior leaders wear multiple hats. Making mistakes is also a natural part of the growth phase and is often referred to as *technical debt*.

However, it's also important to recognize that some decisions can have significant consequences for the business, and it's essential to minimize the risk of making bad decisions as much as possible. In some cases, mistakes can lead to irreversible damage to the business, or the loss of important resources such as time, money or talent.

The key to success is not necessarily avoiding mistakes altogether, but rather being able to learn from them quickly and adapt your approach accordingly. This requires a culture of openness and transparency, where leaders feel comfortable acknowledging gaps in their knowledge and working collaboratively with external leaders who have trodden the path already.

Ultimately, the most successful startups are those where the executives are able to strike a balance between agility and prudence, taking calculated risks while minimizing the potential downsides. This requires a combination of strong leadership, clear communication, and a willingness to learn from both success and failure.

The 10×Generation mindset not only embraces a culture of experimentation and a focus on customer needs, but is also prepared to pivot quickly as soon as the organization has achieved momentum.

Small-to-medium business

In the SMB organization, we start to see a larger executive structure that has more individuals brought in to manage a growing concern. At the SMB level, the executive is more adept at leadership and has more understanding of what is needed at a strategic level. However, there is still a lack of understanding across all tiers, and this disconnect is felt when decision-making is at the core of the strategic tier.

Organizational structure at this point can become top-heavy, and creating additional layers in the executive will impact overall visibility and communication across the organization. In the upcoming scene, we focus on structure and the best way to manage a growing business.

Act 3, Scene 5: Structured for success

#Startup #Scaleup #SMB #LargeEnterprise

#Tactical #Strategic

The organization has brought in a new CTO to manage all of the IT in the business. The CEO, having a lack of understanding of the technology organization, decides that the best way to manage the increasing costs of technology is to have the CTO report into the CFO. This way, costs in the technology space can be controlled.

The lights come up on our stage, where we see the CTO hunched over a laptop, looking dejected and worried. In walks the CFO with a printout in hand, which she then throws onto the CTO's desk.

Narrator	When the CTO joined the enterprise, it was made clear that the role would be reporting directly into the CFO. The CEO was adamant that costs in the technology space needed to be accounted for and that the ever-increasing costs and requests for new technology, more people and more space could no longer be accommodated.
CFO (Lakshmi)	Is this another business case for approval?
CTO (Jane)	I inherited a pretty decent budget and now I need to spend some of it. It doesn't make any sense to me that I need to provide a full business case every time I need to spend some of the already agreed budget.

This is becoming ridiculous. I'm up to my 16th iteration of this business case. |

CFO (Lakshmi)	I understand that you inherited this budget, but the processes are in place so that I have greater visibility of the spend across the technology function.
	I need to know where the money is going and what the return on investment is going to be. Your predecessor was not transparent, and the spend got out of control.
	We need to show that we're treating money wisely, that's all. I have to show that we're following an auditable path for all of our spend.
	I'm not trying to stonewall you here, Jane.
CTO (Jane)	When I first started, you assured me that my budget was mine to use as I saw fit. What has changed? How do we work better together to make sure you're getting what you need and I'm getting what I need?
CFO (Lakshmi)	If the CEO doesn't see greater velocity from your team, then additional funding is going to be the challenge. We have been burned before, which is why the process is so rigid.
CTO (Jane)	I see. Lakshmi, the challenge we're facing is that we're working with legacy systems that need basic maintenance to keep the lights on. As the systems age, they need more support.
	We need to uplift the systems, which will have cost implications, and also invest in keeping the business operating. It's a double-edged sword. The ROI is hard to achieve, but if we continue to kick the can down the road, eventually we'll be spending a lot more and will be impacted by poor performance.
CFO (Lakshmi)	I didn't realize that this is the problem we face. I've had nothing to do with technology until reporting lines changed and you started with us.
	I need to focus on ROI and cost-saving measures with the CEO. If investment is needed, then we just have to justify it.
CTO (Jane)	And I need to keep this place operating.
Narrator	Our CTO began the conversation feeling exasperated and unsupported, but as the conversation unfolded the impacts of burdensome financial requirements led to a meeting of the minds. The lack of understanding of the technology landscape at the C-suite level is preventing the operational layer being able to do its work, which is impacting the technical layer.
	With a pure focus on ROI and decreasing costs, the lack of investment in technology is also impacting customers.

10×Generation

Burdensome process and micro-management of the technology budget has increasing impacts on the enterprise organization. Lack of investment in people and technology resources impacts the technology function's ability to deliver greater throughput to the organization. This has a cyclical effect: lesser investment breeds decreased velocity.

A lack of understanding of the technology landscape, and of visibility across the operational, tactical and strategic layers, creates distrust and a need for greater justification on IT spend.

From a 10×Generation viewpoint, the solution to a lack of visibility at the strategic level is the process of building trust and having team members reporting into the right levels. The following list provides avenues of approach to address the structure and enable greater visibility:

- Bring together the operational, tactical and strategic team members to work 'side by side'
- Technology leaders need a seat at the C-suite table and on the board. IT is not only an enabler; it is the place where strategy will come to life, and it needs to be heard
- All C-suite members need to have visibility from the top down of all layers, with a view of the pain points
- Budgets that are agreed to are not gathered in isolation. The C-suite is privy to the IT budget and the need for it, and how it will support greater reliability and velocity
- Once budgets are set and greater visibility across the organization is restored, the endless need for business cases ceases.

When costs are the only factor being considered, there is the potential for cost-cutting measures to impact quality. In many organizations, quality is a measure relating to outputs from delivery. In a technology organization, it will relate to the quality of the features being released into production systems. Quality, however, is a measure that should be considered across the organization, and in the next scene relates to the quality of candidates being brought into it. The wrong hire can have as detrimental an impact on a team and organization as a failed feature being deployed or a loss of market share.

Act 3, Scene 6: Costs and quality are not mutually exclusive

#SMB #Enterprise #LargeEnterprise

#Operational #Strategic

The head of P&C is in charge of sourcing and assisting with the hiring and retention of top talent. She has been tasked with reducing recruitment costs. The organization has been using regionally based recruitment companies in an effort to recruit more efficiently, but the cost of using them is being scrutinized.

The lights go up; we find ourselves in a large boardroom.

The head of P&C (Swaty) is meeting with department heads in her organization. All attendees are intently listening to the new strategic direction in which Swaty wants to take the organization's recruiting function.

Narrator	We see the head of P&C presenting her strategic roadmap for the department heads. She is very excited about the direction in which she would like to take recruitment, and has been preparing the slide deck for the last week.
	She has socialized her ideas for reducing recruitment costs with the CEO and CFO, and they are very pleased with her proposed approach.
	Swaty believes that, with the proposed changes, she can reduce recruitment costs by more than 50%. With the ever-increasing requests for headcount across the organization and especially the technology department, a cost saving in recruitment would be a welcome change.
Head of P&C (Swaty)	Thank you all for attending.
	As you know, each of us has been tasked with finding ways of reducing costs in our departments. As the head of the people and culture team, I am looking at ways of continuing to support each of your departments while reducing costs.
	I know that this seems counterintuitive, but I think I may have a solution, which I'm very excited to share with you.

A slide deck is shared on the main screen in the boardroom.

Head of P&C (Swaty)	I've been reviewing all of our past recruitment costs, and I believe that if we insource the recruitment activity, we'll be able to save more than 50% on current costs.
	My team have capacity to pick this work up, and we won't need any additional headcount.
	This really is a win-win scenario.
	The purpose of this meeting is to take each of you through this proposal and gain your feedback.

A slight grumbling can be heard from the meeting attendees as they digest this proposal.

Head of technology (Mike)	Swaty, I understand the need for cost-cutting, but I have some concerns.
	In the technology area, we're experiencing higher demand than we've ever had before.
	The recruiters we use are able to source team members globally, which means we're not limited to a local talent pool. They understand technical recruitment, know the questions to ask and have been working side by side with us to bring in the best talent we can afford.
	I understand what you're trying to achieve – I'm just not sure your team have the right capabilities to be able to support tech recruitment.
Head of P&C (Swaty)	I understand your concerns, Mike, but I think my team can do this. We've been watching the recruiters, and we think that, with the right training and systems, we can support you in just the same way.
Head of customer service (Krish)	Swaty, from a customer service perspective, I think this is a great idea. We don't need specialist recruiters for the entry-level roles. I think your team could really be a great support and much more cost effective for me.
Head of product (Roberto)	From a product perspective, I agree with Mike. We need specialist recruiters with a large talent database to draw on.
	I can see your cost savings, Swaty, but have you considered time as a variable in your measures? If it takes your team three times as long, there is a cost impact that you haven't taken into account.
Head of P&C (Swaty)	I really appreciate your feedback, gents. I'm asking you this: what would it take to make this work?
	How can I convince you that this is a viable option for us?
Head of technology (Mike)	I think you need to listen to what we're saying. To undertake product and technology recruitment, your team needs a specialist skill set.
	Perhaps you could look at bringing someone in-house that meets that need. You'd need to consider having someone in each region, or with contacts in other regions, to widen the talent pool.
Head of P&C (Swaty)	*(Exasperated)* But that would increase the costs and defeat the purpose. There has to be a better way …
Head of product (Roberto)	Why not try piloting your option with the entry level positions, like Krish mentioned? There would be cost savings there – just not as much to start with. Trial this to see if it works, then broaden it to other teams.

Head of P&C (Swaty)	But I've already promised these savings!
Head of technology (Mike)	Swaty, I understand what you're saying, but cost and quality are not mutually exclusive. We have to ensure the talent we bring in helps and doesn't hinder our progress.
	We cannot afford to destabilize the teams with the wrong hires. The most important thing we do when we recruit is work towards hiring the best talent that works well in our business. This can't just be a cost-saving exercise, otherwise it will cost much more in the long term.
Narrator	The meeting ends, with Swaty feeling disappointed that she was unable to get agreement across the departments.

10×Generation

When individual departments are given goals that do not marry up with those of other departments, we start to see misalignment. In this scenario, we have the people and culture team wanting to employ cost-cutting measures, as this is a target that is expected in that department.

However, when leaders want to make this change, there needs to be greater consultation. If they focus only on the one area and do not have a clear vision as to how the change will impact other departments, we see decisions being made that have a negative impact overall.

Unless every department has similar or complementary measures embedded in its success criteria, we will see disparity across the organization.

The solution to departmental misalignment is as follows:

- Have the same key measures embedded across all departments. In this scenario, if cost-cutting was also part of the operational layer, it is entirely possible that the way in which technology recruits would be considered and a two-way conversation between HR and IT would take place. By working together towards a common goal, both departments would meet the overall objective
- Take the concept of business partnering a step further by having business advocates whose primary function is to advocate for the team they support
- Link monetary rewards, such as bonuses, to the ways the departments work together. Have key success criteria determined to ensure that the ways of working can be measured.

Act 3, Scene 7: Missed it by this much …

#Scaleup #SMB #Enterprise #LargeEnterprise

#Operational #Tactical #Strategic

In an SMB organization, sometimes a missed deliverable can derail your entire marketing strategy, impact your customer base or severely impact your ability to raise funding to support your growth targets. When there are many dependencies across the organization, but a lack of cohesion between key layers, we see impactful events that have the power to shock your business.

Let's see what happens when senior leaders divorce themselves from driving strategic initiatives and decide what they feel is important to the business without consultation.

Our scene opens with a heated discussion among three senior leaders in the organization. Each of them represents an impacted area of the business.

Narrator	We join the CMO, CIO and CPO, who are liberally discussing a pressing release needed to drive a market-changing feature for the organization.
	We soon learn that the feature is not ready, as key teams were not consulted at the start of the development process, and now there is a very real possibility that the release will be delayed. If it is, the external optics will have significant ramifications for the business – greater than any of the senior leaders realize.
CMO (Alexandra)	Ajay, the tech team have advised that our new feature is ready from a technical perspective but there are concerns with the stability of the platform. I thought your quality team were all over this?
CIO (Ajay)	It has nothing to do with the quality team, Alexandra. The issue is that the product team have changed requirements mid-development and haven't confirmed that these meet the business need.
CPO (Alec)	Don't blame my team for your team's lack of delivery!
CMO (Alexandra)	Hang on a minute. What has changed? We had clear requirements at the start of this project, and we've run the marketing campaign to support this feature set.
	Alec, what has been changed?
CPO (Alec)	During the development stage, we decided to make changes to the user interface to make the product better.

CMO (Alexandra)	I thought we were going with a limited scope to meet the time lines and would iterate based on the VOC feedback? We've communicated this to Ken and the board.
CPO (Alec)	The product team knows what's best for this feature, and we've done exactly that.
CMO (Alexandra)	I understand what you're saying, Alec, but who did you advise?

There is a pregnant pause as Alec stares angrily at Alexandra and Ajay.

CPO (Alec)	This isn't my team's fault. We've done what's best for the business. Ajay, your team just needs to make this happen. This is really important to the business.
CIO (Ajay)	Alec, we're now down a completely different pathway, and the deliverables can't be met in the available timeframe. What we presented to the regulatory bodies has been changed, and we can't take this back for approval in its current state.
CPO (Alec)	Then we need to throw more people at the problem. More people, greater velocity!
CIO (Ajay)	Development doesn't work like that, Alec.
Narrator	Our scene ends with the leaders at an impasse.

We now enter the CEO's office, where a serious discussion is taking place regarding the new feature.

CEO (Ken)	That new feature is the turning point for this organization, Lakshmi.
CFO (Lakshmi)	Ken, if we don't get this out into the wild, we don't have enough run rate to continue trading past the next two quarters.
CEO (Ken)	I've been speaking with the VOC team, and they've made it very clear: if this doesn't go out on time, they'll be looking at replacing our management team and forcing us to restructure.

The CPO, CMO and CIO enter the CEO's office.

CMO (Alexandra)	Ken, sorry to interrupt, but we have a bit of an issue.
	It looks like the feature set we promised to the market is going to miss the timelines promised.
Narrator	The CEO and CFO's faces lose all colour, and they stare at each other.
	Their worst nightmare is about to unfold in front of them.
	With no options presented to meet the deliverables, the organization is in significant trouble.

10×Generation

When an organization has a clearly defined strategy, it must be communicated to all levels. The strategy defines the direction for the organization and the underpinning ways of working.

In the 10×Generation state, an individual's or team's own perception of what is required does not override the importance of the strategy. Collaboration, understanding and communication are vital in ensuring that all activity in the organization is aligned with its needs.

Visibility is achieved by implementing the 10×Generation principles, which enables cohesion across the organization. It lends itself to a culture of knowing, not a culture of assumptions. When assumptions are replaced with facts and strategic intent, there is a sense of certainty across the organization that all deliverables will be achieved as communicated. Without this alignment, no one is ever certain of outcomes, and presumption becomes the way of operating.

When enough significant deliverables are missed, there may be a point when an organization is impacted by a potential acquisition. Sometimes this is necessary for growth, and sometimes it is hostile in nature. Regardless of the type of acquisition, there will be ways to thrive during the process.

Act 3, Scene 8: Acquisition alchemy – how to thrive during an acquisition process

#Scaleup #SMB

#Strategic

It's easy to be the acquirer during an acquisition – but what if you are being acquired? Generally, the project will have a code name and you will be among the very few who know what the organization is about to embark on.

Being acquired can be a challenging process, especially if you are going through multiple due diligence (DD) procedures. DD is a critical part of the acquisition process. It's important to be prepared to provide the acquiring company with all the necessary information and documentation it needs to assess the value of your business.

In the scenario below, we will see the most common mistakes in planning: not involving the right people, focusing on the wrong areas, not addressing integration issues, and rushing the process.

We open on a tense scene in a conference room. A group of executives from the acquiring company, led by the stern and focused group CEO, sit at one end of a long table. At the other end sit the executives of the target company, including the team working on the DD and the mediating company that helps with all the data. It looks like a scene from the TV series Succession; *if you have not watched this one, you should.*

Narrator	We have a group of senior leaders from both companies who are all focused on ensuring that the DD is a clear, no-nonsense process and does not waste time.
CEO of acquirer (John)	Let's have a quick round of introductions, and then I want to go through the due diligence checklist, starting with financials, followed by technology.
Narrator	It is clear that many individuals in both organizations take great pride in their introductions and have quite an inflated sense of self-importance.
	As John begins to question the CFO of the acquirer (Jean) about the target company's financials, we see glimpses of the mistakes being made throughout the process.
	Jean struggles to answer the questions about financials, stumbling over numbers and details. We see a shot of John exchanging a concerned look with his colleagues.
CFO of acquirer (Jean)	I'll find the numbers and data that you've asked for and share them in the [code name] Slack room.
CTO (Jane)	Let me start by giving you an overview of our tech stack and a high-level view of all my departments.
Narrator	There is a ten-minute, 30,000-foot-view explanation by Jane. She struggles to answer the CTO and other senior technology people's questions about the target technology company's development process, stumbling over technical details.
CTO of acquirer (Denzel)	*(To Jane)* Who did you involve in this part of the process?

Flashback to international technology company – weeks earlier.

Jane sits with a few colleagues in a meeting room, discussing due diligence. Jane is making notes, and makes the executive decision of not inviting some of the key people for the DD calls, as they have not been in her good books.

Back to the conference room.

CTO (Jane)	*(Starts fluffing around other topics and tries to avoid the question; closes with the following)* We are all technical people, so we focused too much on development processes and not enough on other areas.
Narrator	Denzel moves on to other areas of due diligence, but the same problems arise. Jane struggles to answer questions about data security, IT infrastructure and other important areas.
	As the due diligence process wears on, tensions rise. The CEO becomes increasingly frustrated with Jane and her team, and they become increasingly defensive.

The scene ends on a shot of Jane and her team exiting the meeting room, leaving the CEO and his team to deal with the aftermath of their mistakes with the executive group.

10×Generation

As an acquiree, there are several best practices to follow during a DD process to ensure that the acquisition goes smoothly and to minimize any potential risks or issues. From a 10×Generation view, this is made easier when there is greater visibility across an organization. Running a lean, streamlined business, however, may impact individuals' day jobs, and this should be considered as you build out the DD team.

Here is the best way to manage the DD process:

- Preparation:
  - Measure twice, cut once.* The challenge is managing the team's time, as this is going to be a second job that very few people in the business are aware of
  - Ensure that the DD process has assembled a team that can efficiently and effectively respond to requests for information from the acquiring company, and is aware of the sensitivity of the request
  - This team should include key resources from every department, such as finance, legal, technology and human resources, to ensure that communications can be managed and the rumour mill can be quietened down when needed

---

*Plan and prepare carefully before taking action.

- Organization:
  - Be organized and systematic in your approach to presenting the information that the acquiring company has requested
  - Provide a clear and concise executive summary
  - Organize the supporting documents in a logical and easy-to-follow manner. Remember that if this acquisition does not go forward, you will have laid the groundwork for others that may potentially arise
- Communication:
  - Establish clear lines of communication with the acquiring company throughout the DD process
  - Ensure all team members involved respond promptly to requests for information
  - Establish a proactive communication process to highlight any issues or concerns that arise, ensuring the process does not stall
- Risk management:
  - Identify potential risks and issues that could arise during the acquisition process, and develop a plan for managing them
  - Include thorough risk assessments and gap analysis, and develop contingency plans for any potential issues
  - Keep a register of the issues and risks, similar to that of a project plan, tracking and addressing as you move through the process
- Post-transaction integration:
  - Develop a plan for integrating the acquiree into the acquiring company's operations
  - Document the integration plan, regardless of whether you think the process will be successful or not. Having an understanding of the integration process can be useful for various scenarios, including situations where you might transition from being the acquirer to the acquiree
  - Identify key personnel, develop a communication plan, and ensure that there is a clear understanding of roles and responsibilities.

In the 10×Generation state, mergers and acquisitions (M&A) are a state of being for many organizations. The difference is that in an organization that is working with a model of visibility, transparency and clearly defined roles and responsibilities, the process is much easier to manage. Having a plan to manage under the pressures of due diligence is something that should be developed as part of the organization's strategy, regardless of its size and maturity.

Enterprise

As covered in Chapter 3 on the tactical view, we will see an increase in size and complication as the executive grows with additional layers. Compared with the SMB organization, at the enterprise level there will be a lot of layers in a tall organizational structure.

This can provide opportunity for layers of advancement – but, in turn, if communication and visibility are not core principles, we will see silos forming and poor work practices impacting overall delivery.

In the next scene we see what happens when ownership turns into control and becomes detrimental to the ongoing efficiencies of the organization.

Act 3, Scene 9: There is no 'I' in 'team'

#SMB #Enterprise #LargeEnterprise

#Tactical #Strategic

When working in the strategic view, there is a need to have access to data across the organization. We find, however, that in large organizations, access to data across departments is not available. There is a lack of data ownership, and this ultimately leads to data being siloed and not being accessible to executive leaders.

Lack of access to relevant data impacts the organization's ability to make insightful decisions and drive the business forward.

Our scene is set at the start of the organization's end-of-financial-year processing. The CMO is meeting with the CEO in the CEO's office to discuss the business intelligence team and the data that is being provided to drive insights into the customer lifetime value reports and customer churn rates.

Narrator	The data that is being provided is not including the financial data needed to understand the impacts on the marketing spend, and this is causing issues for the CMO. She has requested greater access to the various teams' data, but this has been withheld.
CEO (Ken)	Alexandra, I don't understand why it's so difficult to report on our customers' lifetime value and retention rates. This information is vital for us to understand whether our product is meeting our customers' needs.
CMO (Alexandra)	Ken, I've been working with the BI team and trying to get this nailed, and, to be honest, it's taking months and I'm still no closer to being able to provide this.
CEO (Ken)	Surely this should be a simple ask?
CMO (Alexandra)	It would be simple if the disparate teams in different departments owned their data and were in control of it. We have so many processes across the data but no one in control of it. There are no decision makers in the departments, so the data being captured is a mess.
CEO (Ken)	We need Kharan in here to tell us what's happening in the data space. He owns this area.

Kharan, the chief data officer (CDO), enters the office.

CEO (Ken)	Kharan, why can't we report on customer lifetime value?
CDO (Kharan)	*(Looking uncomfortable)* Sorry, Ken, what do you mean?
CEO (Ken)	Well, I have Alexandra here telling me that she's unable to report on important areas in her department because the data isn't available to her.
	This is your job, isn't it? You own all the data, right?
CDO (Kharan)	That isn't entirely true, Ken.
	I own the data platform and the processes to collect, manage and store data, but I don't have ownership of the data. Each department needs to own the data, how it's classified and how it's updated, and advise what they require to be ingested into the data warehouse.
	If this isn't provided to my team and we don't know what's required, we can't provide it.
CMO (Alexandra)	You see what I mean, Ken? No one has ownership of the data, and I can't get what I need to understand this key marketing metric.

The CEO looks frustrated.

CDO (Kharan)	Ken, we need to have data ownership embedded in the business otherwise I am not going to be able to provide you with what you and Alexandra need.

Cut to the CFO's office.

CFO (Lakshmi)	I don't understand what you mean by 'data ownership', Kharan.
	I have my financial reports and my team need to access these. I don't particularly want anyone else having access to my data. I have all of the organization's financials, and I don't want anyone accessing this stuff if they don't have to.
CDO (Kharan)	Part of data ownership is having the authority to make changes to ensure data quality – things like cleansing the data and running data audits. You own it and determine who can access it.
	We need to have data ownership in place, otherwise we're going to continue to keep running into these issues.
CFO (Lakshmi)	I'll think about it. For now, I own my own data and I really don't want anyone else accessing it except for my team of analysts.

CDO (Kharan)	This will impact our ability to provide the reports that Alexandra needs, Lakshmi.
Narrator	Our meeting ends in an impasse.
	The CDO cannot persuade the CFO to release data, therefore the CMO will not have her reports.
	Without these valuable insights, the business will not be able to determine how best to retain its customers.

10×Generation

In the 10×Generation state, teams work collectively for the benefit of the organization. Strategies are developed at each tier, and link together to form an overarching strategic intent that the entire organization has visibility and buy-in to.

There is ownership, but this is not at the expense of collaboration and the betterment of the organization.

Ego is parked to the side; the command-and-control approach is a thing of the past and not tolerated in the 10×Generation state.

It should be noted that while collaboration and sharing are essential, they do not negate the need for security-related governance and controls. However, these measures are not intended to hinder overall progress within the organization.

In working with the organization to understand governance and control, the next step is having knowledge of the executive's risk appetite. Let's see what happens when this is unclear.

Act 3, Scene 10: Determining risk appetite

#Startup #Scaleup #SMB #Enterprise #LargeEnterprise

#Operational #Tactical #Strategic

The enterprise organization has been impacted by a significant natural disaster that has brought down a major data centre. The technology function had sought funding to support offsite backups and a disaster recovery location, but this was determined to be too costly by the business stakeholders.

The stage is set with the group CIO, CEO and CFO sitting at the boardroom table. All look exhausted, with laptops open and a slide presentation on the boardroom screen. A major flood has just taken down the business's main data centre. The offsite backups were still not in place, and the facility is under 6 feet of floodwater. All business-critical systems are offline and the business has ground to a halt.

Narrator	When the last budgets were set, the group CIO and CEO met to discuss the need to shore up the primary data centre. A number of disaster scenarios were highlighted in the last external audit, and the CIO wanted to be able to address these and satisfy the audit findings.
	The CFO and CEO had requested that all budgets be halved where possible, and technology spend was no exception.
	They also decided to slow down some of the audit initiatives in order to save some money. The CIO was adamant that the most important thing was addressing the audit outcomes, but was overruled.
	The CFO and CEO believed that the business could wait until the next financial year for disaster failover and offsite backups. This was an insurance policy after all, and could be pushed out. The risk appetite of the business was high, and the spend could wait.
CEO (Ken)	How bad is the impact of this flood?
CIO (Ajay)	Our main business-critical systems were in that data centre. Backup servers were there as well. One of our smaller data centres received the backup tape drives from the primary data centre two weeks ago.
CFO (Lakshmi)	So, what does that mean?
CIO (Ajay)	We have a backup from two weeks ago, but have lost all data and transactions since then.
	We've sourced a version of the business-critical system at another data centre, but we'll be offline for at least two weeks while we get back up and operating.
	We've lost all financial data for the last two weeks, and our operational teams are running manually with paper-based backup processes.
CEO (Ken)	I don't understand how we could be in this situation. I thought we backed everything up?
CIO (Ajay)	Do you recall when we discussed addressing the findings from our last audit?

Both the CEO and CFO nod.

CIO (Ajay)	I requested the funding to make provision for offsite automated backups, and funding to have a disaster recovery location. It was decided in that meeting that we could wait and push this activity out until the next budgeting period.

CFO (Lakshmi)	This is a disaster. It's going to cost us a fortune!
CIO (Ajay)	Now we are here, and this is worse than we thought it could be.
Narrator	It is only when a major disaster befalls this organization that it realizes the importance of the technology spend and addressing audit findings as soon as possible.

10×Generation

Cost-cutting of the IT budget is a by-product of a lack of visibility as to why the spend is necessary. In the 10×Generation world, visibility is available at all layers, and the importance of the work needed to secure the organization is clearly understood.

All layers understand the need for disaster recovery practices. The development, training and support that is needed to embed this is a key pillar to support the level of understanding in the business.

Budgets should not be held to ransom when an organization is underperforming.

Major natural disasters can be better managed if the strategic leadership understands the need for maintenance and new technologies.

The solution to continued ransom of budgets is as follows:

- Risk appetite in an organization is agreed and understood at all levels. When a disaster happens, everyone is aware of their responsibilities, and blame should never enter into the conversation
- A disaster mitigation strategy is communicated to all, not siloed to the technology department only. In the 10×Generation world, everyone has visibility and accountability, and everyone has a say. Just as with a business continuity plan, everyone needs to be aware of this
- Disasters will impact all layers; therefore a level of visibility as to the importance of mitigation must be communicated and embraced
- If a team is responsible for business continuity planning or disaster recovery, these duties are clearly outlined in the team members' job descriptions.

If an organization's executive team collaborates and understands the consequences and steps required for recovery in the event of a disaster, the organization is better prepared to mitigate the impact of a catastrophe. When cost-cutting efforts target budgets and neglect foundational components, organizations are often severely impacted when these foundational services fail.

Act 3, Scene 11: The power of the purse – a board's guide to budgeting for success

#SMB #Enterprise #LargeEnterprise

#Strategic

In all organizations, regardless of their size or maturity, there will always be a budgeting process where each member of the senior leadership team needs to state their case for more funding. In this next scene, we see a conversation between the CIO and the organization's board. Let's see how the CIO tries to explain the need for more budget to support the organization's ageing infrastructure, the rapid rate of technology change and the need to invest more in cybersecurity.

Curtain rises and lights go up.

We find ourselves in a large boardroom, with a table laden with breakfast food, coffee and tea paraphernalia, and board papers.

The board members are meeting for the annual budget review, and each senior leader enters the room.

Picture a scene from Oliver Twist, *with each leader skulking into the boardroom, cap in hand, requesting their funding …*

Narrator	Our next participant in the funding tango is the CIO, who needs to seek additional funding well above the previous year's budget.
	It will be a contentious discussion, as the board is looking at avenues for trimming the budget in preparation for the annual report to shareholders.
Board chairperson	Please welcome Ajay, our chief information officer, to the floor.
CIO (Ajay)	Thank you, everyone. I've shared my budget figures prior to this meeting. I'm here to answer any questions regarding the next year's budget for the technology department.
Board member A	Thank you, Ajay.
	We've gone through the budget request and we have quite a few questions in relation to it.
	Firstly, this is a 40% increase on last year's budget, which is quite substantial. Are you able to advise this board what has changed in one year to necessitate such a large investment in the technology department? After all, we're not a technology company.

Board member B	I'd also like to understand the reasons behind the significant increase in cybersecurity needs. As previously mentioned, we aren't a technology company, so cybersecurity risks aren't typically a primary concern for us.
CIO (Ajay)	I understand the board's reluctance to increase the IT budget, but there are some harsh realities that must be called out.
	We have ageing infrastructure that needs to be uplifted, to ensure our security and to enable us to provide reliable technology to support the entire business.
	Although we're not a technology company *per se*, all companies are technology companies. Technology is the backbone of the organization, and it must be supportable and reliable.
	We also capture customer data, and it's important to ensure that this is kept secure as well as ensuring that our internal systems are kept secure.
	I can't manage this and the rate of change in the technology space with the current budget, so I've requested an increase.
Board member B	Ajay, this is a surprising request. We haven't been kept in the loop at all in relation to the ever-increasing costs of IT, and this budget request is going to be extremely hard to justify to our shareholders.
	It almost feels like this board is being blindsided by this request. Why didn't we hear about this earlier?
Board chairperson	IT isn't generally asked to present to the board. As it's known that we're not a technology company, it hasn't been deemed important.
Board member B	I just don't understand how IT costs could have escalated this much. This makes no sense to me, and I'm not in favour of increasing this budget at this time. We have shareholders to report to, and this type of uncontrolled expense will send red flags to the market.
CIO (Ajay)	Without this increase, our IT is at risk.
Board member C	This type of hysterical attitude isn't what we need from a C-suite executive, Ajay. I think you need to go back to your budget from last year and look at what can be done with a 5% increase in costs.
Narrator	The CIO exits the boardroom realizing that the budget he had painstakingly put together has been rejected and it is unlikely he will receive any more than what was approved in the previous year.
	What could Ajay have done differently?
	Our scene ends with a disgruntled CIO and a business at possible risk.

10×Generation

In the 10×Generation state, the communication lines between the operational, tactical and strategic views extend to that of the board. The board is an extension of the strategic view, as its members are also key decision makers in the organization.

As Deloitte has mentioned,[48] having a tech-savvy board is an absolute need when having budgeting conversations. When technology is not understood in its entirety, we find missed opportunities for organizations to increase market share, increased risk of cyberattacks, and potential issues with scalability and supportability across the organization.

Board members are embedded into the 10×Generation state in the same way as all other members of the organization, and are set organizational goals in the same way as all other roles. The board's obligations do not stop at strategic governance and oversight, serving the organization's stakeholders, managing budgets, setting policies, overseeing personnel, setting goals, and measuring goals and achievements.[49] In the 10×Generation state, they also include having a broad understanding of each layer and how it operates to ensure that the strategic oversight is adhered to across each tier.

Act 3, Scene 12: The acquirer's playbook – winning at M&A

#SMB #Enterprise #LargeEnterprise

#Strategic

To conclude the strategic view and the three acts, we now play out the company's acquisition – one of the most common scenarios for a successful business. For what is bigger than being an acquirer in the global M&A market? According to a report by Statista,[50] the total value of global M&A deals amounted to US$5.9 trillion in 2021 and US$3.8 trillion in 2022. There are quite a few challenges when you are the company that needs to perform due diligence: financial considerations, regulatory hurdles, integration issues, legal complexities.

In general, most of these common scenarios would already be covered by your playbook. The greater challenge lies in having a clear perspective and objective, and comprehending the purpose of the acquisition as an organization. If there are numerous leaders, each having their viewpoint on the perceived value of the acquisition, this can further complicate matters.

The following scenario highlights the point that in the M&A process, leaders' opinions and preconceived notions may take precedence over the organization's needs and objectives, much like conducting an interview where the questions asked do not align with the job description. This can lead to a less effective evaluation of potential acquisitions.

Curtain rises and lights go up.

A team of executives are gathered around a conference table. Among them are the group CEO (who heads the entire organization and leads the regional CEOs), the CFO, CTO and CPO, and the head of strategy.

Group CEO (Pratesh)	Well, team, it looks like we've got a potential acquisition on our hands!
CPO (Alec)	Really? That's great news.
CTO (Jane)	*(Excitedly)* What's the company?
Group CEO (Pratesh)	Well, the project is code-named 'Elon', and the company we're talking about is a tech startup that's been making waves in the industry. They've got some innovative products and a strong market share.
Head of strategy (Oscar)	Can we ensure going forward we use the code name in discussions when referring to this company?
CPO (Alec)	*(Sceptically)* But do we really need to acquire them? What value will they bring to our organization?
Head of strategy (Oscar)	*(Leaning forward)* I think they could help us expand our reach and get a foothold in some new markets.
Group CEO (Pratesh)	*(Nodding)* Exactly. But before we make any decisions, we need to conduct a thorough due diligence process to make sure they're the right fit for us.
Narrator	As they begin to discuss their due diligence process, they quickly realize they don't really know what questions they should be asking. Given they are running out of time, they decide to proceed and engage in a deep dive with the possible prospects.

Cut to present day: check-in call after the DD process.

Group CEO (Pratesh)	Team, thanks for your time today. How do you think that went?
CPO (Alec)	I'm not sure the questions we asked were getting us the information we need.
CFO (Lakshmi)	*(Dismissively)* Oh, I think we're doing just fine. We have a good grasp on the company's financials and operations.

Head of strategy (Oscar)	Yes, I agree. We've already uncovered some key data points that will help us make a strong case for the acquisition.
Narrator	Despite their lack of understanding, all but Alec continue to pat each other on the back and congratulate themselves on their progress.

In the above scenario, it's clear that the teams performing the DD are unaware of the crucial information they're missing and the potential risks of proceeding without a thorough evaluation. One of the possible ways to perform DDs could be to ask for external advice or to incorporate the appropriate talent.

10×Generation

Mergers and acquisitions (M&As) are no small feat, due to the complexity, high stakes, costs and risks involved in the process. They require careful planning, execution and management to ensure a successful outcome. They typically involve a range of activities, including due diligence (DD), valuation, negotiations, legal and regulatory compliance, and post-merger integration.

For both the acquirer and the acquiree, M&As can be incredibly difficult and time-consuming. There are often many moving parts and stakeholders involved, including executives, legal teams, accountants, financial advisers and regulatory agencies. Coordinating all of these parties and ensuring that everyone is on the same page can be a daunting task.

If the deal goes through successfully, it can lead to significant growth and value creation for both companies. However, if the deal falls through or is not executed effectively, it can result in significant financial losses and damage to the reputations of the companies involved.

In the 10×Generation state, bringing in the right talent can also mean bringing in the right consultant. DD firms specialize in conducting thorough and effective due diligence. They bring a wealth of experience and expertise to the process, which can help identify potential risks and opportunities that an internal team might miss.

This option lets the internal teams focus on business-as-usual activities and more critical aspects of the M&A process. One of the biggest advantages is that they can provide an objective perspective on the target company, without being influenced by internal politics or biases.

If executed well, the M&A process can help a company achieve its strategic goals, create value for shareholders and drive long-term growth.

Epilogue

In the 36 scenarios provided, there are solutions and ideas about what the 10×Generation state could be in your organization. Whatever level you are at in the organization, you should have a voice. You should have visibility of what is happening and where you fit into the company's growth aspirations.

Many individuals seek out this level of visibility and autonomy, and decide to work in a startup. This is demanding work, but the outcomes, if the organization is a success, are worth the effort. How amazing would it be to work in an SMB or enterprise and feel the same way you felt working in a startup?

If you transform your organization to the 10×Generation state, it is entirely possible to recreate the startup feel and outputs, and to win market share. The transition is not going to be easy, as you propel your way into a different operating model, but the outcomes could be extraordinary for all.

8 Transforming to the 10×Generation state – embedding the principles

To transform your organization to the 10×Generation state, it will take thorough planning and a commitment from all tiers of your organization. The 10×Generation state is a new way of working and will challenge the thinking across your business. It will require a solid programme to make this a sustainable change that will ensure your continued controlled growth and operational efficiencies.

In each act in Chapter 7, we provided scenarios where the 10×Generation principles (EA³) are not known and organizations are impacted; each scenario includes ideas for you to consider. Many readers will find that they experience many of the scenarios regularly; however, the intention was not to provide a prescriptive approach to resolving them.

There are multiple combinations of resolutions, and each combination depends on the size of the organization, its level of maturity, the individuals involved, embedded ways of working and the overall culture. To provide authoritative resolutions would go against the premise of what the 10×Generation state represents, and would never address the multitude of permutations that exist.

The 10×Generation state is one of open communication, visibility both horizontally and vertically, empowerment and cohesion aligning with the organization's strategic vision. We have provided guidelines, but the implementation of the 10×Generation state is as varied as the organizations that would benefit from it. The advice provided will start you on your journey to an ideal state, with ideas and options, some that can be easily adopted and others that will take considerable effort.

The first step will be to focus on embedding the 10×Generation principles.

In Act 1, we focused on the issues that are faced when working in the operational layer of an organization that is burdened with old organizational design theory (see box in Chapter 6 on 'What is organizational design theory?'). Whether you find yourself in a flat structure, meaning fewer management levels, or a tall structure with greater command and control, there are ways of transforming to reflect the 10×Generation state.

When the operational view is not aligned with the tactical and strategic views, the organization will be burdened by unproductive silos, a lack of visibility and a lack of united decision-making, as our scripts demonstrated. Some silos are of benefit; however, when they become obstructionist, this is when problems arise. All functions in the organization desperately seek to work together, but without the underpinning 10×Generation principles to adhere to, the same conversations and problems will continue to arise.

In Acts 2 and 3, we focused on the departmental and executive views. Each scenario was based on the problems that are experienced at all tiers in an organization. The context may shift and the language may change, but the outcomes will remain the same if a new way of operating is not found.

To ensure that each layer is able to function cohesively, all tiers across the organization must adopt the 10×Generation principles. However, before you embark on this programme, you will need to discern your organization's current ways of working. Through gaining a clear understanding of the key dependencies that may impact a change programme, and the gaps you have, you will be able to build out your change plan, focusing on the four principles. There is no magic bullet to this step in the process. This is just something that must be done to ensure that every gap and dependency is understood and addressed. When assumptions are made that prove to be incorrect, they have the potential to derail progress. At times, the only option is to revert to past processes in order to move forward.

Embedding the first principle: Empowerment

The first principle, empowerment, looks across the entire organization, regardless of role or embedded hierarchy. When empowerment is the foundation, innovation has the freedom to accelerate any organization's growth and vision. Innovation is not owned solely by technology; innovation of thought is owned by all.

The ideas provided here are not exhaustive, but they are designed to get you thinking about the specific initiatives you can undertake to get you on your journey. The empowerment principle is made up of three key elements that will bring the principle to life.

Accountability and ownership

This sounds simple enough, but so often is put to the side. Leaders who believe that they have all the answers tend to micro-manage teams in an effort to ensure deliverables are met, resulting in the opposite taking place. A disempowered workforce is the worst outcome any organization faces. When so much of what we do relies on discretionary effort, a workforce that does not own its destiny is crippled by clock-watching and a lack of inspiration.

Here are some ways to ingrain accountability and ownership:

- Revisit position or job descriptions to ensure role clarity for all. These do not need to be onerous, but need to have clear accountabilities and ownership documented and agreed on. They should be updated regularly, in agreement with employees,* as the organization grows

- Make all role objectives visible to all: no secrets; everything is open for comment. Roles may have slightly different objectives, which would fly in the face of the tradition of having a single job description for a set of roles. Individual job descriptions can have overarching similarities, but objectives may vary, and need to be made visible to all

- Ensure success measures are agreed on at the individual, team and organizational levels. They should be tracked and visible to all

- Gamify the success measures, to ensure greater buy-in and create a healthy competition among teams. Be sure to monitor the competition aspect to ensure that strategic goals are a key focus. When everyone is working towards the strategic goals, this will create cohesion in their efforts.

Open communication

In so many organizations, there is a reluctance to communicate openly. This is indicative of a culture that does not trust the employees to be the holders of information. In the 10×Generation state, communication is about empowering people with the right information to make informed decisions. This is not about giving away state secrets, but about telling teams what they need to know in order to succeed. There will be times when not all information can be shared; however, information related to the ability of team members to meet strategic initiatives should be communicated, where practicable.

The rituals and ways of communicating provide every individual with a clear view of the strategy in their team, in their tier and across the organization.

Here are the options that can get you started:

- Implement open forums or ceremonies for continuous dialogue, put the ground rules in place and ensure that everyone has a platform for their opinion, creating an environment where people feel heard. Create a setting of respectful challenge, where ideas are discussed openly. Specific forums may include:
  - Anonymous forums enabling open communication, providing a safe space for all to say what they feel
  - TechAnon – an open technical forum that includes product and technology team members working side by side
  - Team huddles – short touchpoints that enable open discussion
  - Team meetings – where company outcomes, team objectives and tracking can be made visible

---

* Where there are unions, this will be performed in consultation with them to ensure an equitable outcome is achieved.

- Document and publish the communication channels, and ensure that access is granted across the organization to information such as strategy updates, using various forms of communication that make the information accessible to all. For example:
  - Company or team blog
  - Update reports
  - Roadmap trackers
  - Podcasts
  - IM channels focused purely on updates
- Ensure that all team leaders are sharing outcomes with each other; the health of individual teams is not a secret
- Enable leaders to use clear and concise communication to explain their rationale for saying 'no' if requests from departments or other leaders are not aligned with the strategic goals. They can offer alternative solutions or suggestions that can help address the underlying issue, but teams and leaders alike are empowered to say 'no'.

Education and knowledge

Many large organizations have a training department. In such cases, access to training may be easier than with smaller organizations. Individuals need to take control of their continued education, and many do. If you work in technology, continual upskilling is almost mandatory.

This element is within the empowerment principle; however, it is more than just a case of sending someone on training. It is about creating a learning culture where leaders in each tier mentor those in the next tier down. Senior executives are given the skills to lead and are empowered to do so. Ensuring that everyone has career choice and educational options is key to this element.

The following options will help to bring the learning culture to life:

- Create a mentoring culture. From the senior leadership level downwards, each leader mentors those in the next tier down
- Make sure senior executives have access to executive coaching, to ensure they are able to coach others
- Set educational targets for personal learning, and for the development and education of others. In the operational state, there should never be a conversation where someone in the strategic layer does not understand something at the operational layer
- Create a learning culture, where education is linked to career progression.

Embedding the second principle: Adaptation

Adaptation in an organization is vital to its continued successful growth. This principle goes beyond the standard practice of organizational design changes. It looks at ways in which decisions are made and how empowered team members manage this undertaking. Without the foundations of empowerment, this second principle is not possible. When the foundations are set, there is little need to measure employee sentiment through the often-ignored 'engagement survey', which can bog down a business and impact momentum. Engagement surveys are a subjective measure, and individual sentiment at the time of responding can skew results and lead to greater disharmony.

We have broken down this second principle into the following three elements.

Curiosity and growth

When an organization is opened up to diversity of thought, curiosity becomes the natural by-product – it is celebrated and embraced. Without a curious workforce, stagnation and complacency become the norm, and this is seen in the organization's inability to deliver successful outcomes.

Growth provides choice in a similar way to the learning culture. Curiosity and growth go hand in hand, but neither is possible without a mind shift in leadership to understand the importance of this element of the adaptation principle.

You can create a focus on this element by implementing these suggestions:

- Promote career progression:
  - Have defined career progression charts where individuals can see what options they have to progress within the organization. With career mapping, be sure to map your organizational pathways, including indicators of success. All individuals, with the right training, should be able to move into any role in the organization if they choose to
  - Make learning and career progression a part of your organization's DNA
  - Implement recognition programmes that reward not only monetarily but also with opportunity
- Develop innovation events to gamify innovation targets, such as:
  - Hack-a-thons (generally known in the technology space, but can include a larger set of teams)
  - Strat-a-thons (more strategic in nature, and linking back to the organization's overarching strategy; inclusive of all departments)
- Implement curiosity task forces:
  - Look for process bottlenecks and work on ways of continually removing them
  - Build a community of practices and take everyone on the journey together
  - Implement cross-functional working groups to reinforce learning and encourage 'outside-the-box' thinking

- Implement innovation forums:
  - Teams can self-start on an innovative idea at any point, and are provided with time to set up an innovation team and get to work. This time comes out of the learning budget, as it enables both learning and innovation
  - Ideas are presented at quarterly catch-ups, and next steps are decided on.

Aligned decision-making

Impactful decisions, once agreed, are made visible to the entire organization. The caveat is that some risk-based decisions may need to have controls put in place because their outcomes could be detrimental to the prosperity of the organization. The rationale behind the decision must include how the decision was made, what options were presented and how the decision links to the organization's strategy. The decision-making process must be transparent and demonstrate the unbiased nature of the decision.

Decisions with an individual or team focus do not need to be published to the entire organization – they need to be made visible to the individual and/or team impacted. If more individuals or teams are impacted, the visibility of the decision will grow. As with all decisions made, they must link to the relevant strategy, whether that be an individual's objectives, a team strategy or the organizational strategy. Alignment is the driving factor in this principle. The following list will help guide organization-wide alignment:

- Develop a delegation-of-authority matrix and publish it across the organization
- Define and implement your governance strategy, which should align with your industry standards
- Keep visible scoreboards of decisions made and upcoming decisions that will impact all teams
- Create kanban or scrum boards at individual team level to provide items that require decision-making, with an understanding of dependencies and due dates, but also provide training to ensure that the practices are used correctly
- If meetings are needed to assist with decision-making, be clear about the agenda and what is being discussed, and stay on topic. Do not allow deviation and personal agendas to get in the way of aligned decision-making.

Value-driven thinking

Every decision in the 10×Generation state is considered in the context of, and aligned with, value-driven thinking. This ensures that the options presented are linked to the organization's strategic intent, regardless of which tier – operational, tactical or strategic – they are proposed from. Value-driven thinking has elements of Lean Six Sigma thinking, which ensures that every decision made has elements of either customer value-add (CVA) or business value-add (BVA). Where a course of action is required, this will have either a CVA or a BVA. If neither exist, then it will be up to the decision makers. Where no value is created, the decision to proceed will be discussed. The publication of the decision outcomes is important to sustain the items in this element:

- For any major change including people, process or practice, there need to be at least three options
- As with aligned decision-making, the options presented must link back to the organizational strategy
- Each option needs to be well researched, with discussion of how it will clearly benefit the organization
- All options must go through a consultative process, to ensure that all affected areas are included in the discussion
- Diversity of thought is key to this element being successful
- All decisions, once made, will be published as per the aligned decision-making process.

Embedding the third principle: Assessment

The assessment principle is where the focus will be on ensuring delivery while keeping reduction of debt at the forefront of your thinking. Once the bloat has been removed from the organization, the key will be to make sure you retain the talent, as you will be working with highly efficient and productive teams. Remembering that you have already embedded the first principle, empowerment, you are now building on it. The third principle is designed to have a cumulative effect and to further empower the individual and the teams.

By embracing quality and value, reducing debt, and increasing staff retention, you will be assured of a workforce that has clearly defined goals and understands the power it brings to the organization in order to achieve its strategy.

Quality and value

The first element in the third principle is the concept of quality and value. It looks at ways of increasing delivery across all teams, regardless of function, by removing the barriers to delivery and old-school thinking about measurement.

You can make consistent delivery part of the culture by aligning quality and value objectives with the principles and making the process of delivery fun:

- Reframe measurement objectives to align with the four principles
- Ensure teams are ultimately self-managed and provided with the skills to do so. Address skills gaps to make sure that self-management is a success
- Gamify team delivery, showing the links to team and organizational strategic outcomes
- If measurements are needed, for example for venture capital hurdles, focus on customer feedback with clearly defined customer success metrics, use of product, increased profit margins and increased market share, as well as standard financial measures such as EBIT (earnings before interest and taxes)
- If there are key metrics in one department, ensure that these cascade onto the bigger picture.

Reduction in debt

The term *debt* in this principle refers to technical and process debt. This is accrued by an organization that focuses only on future goals, and does not consider the impacts of rapid growth and the shortcuts made to achieve it. Improvement and waste reduction must become a cultural attribute, and this is only achieved when decisions consider debt removal as part of the underpinning strategy.

If an organization implements these options, debt reduction will become part of the way it operates:

- Rely on the aligned decision-making and value-driven actions to ensure that the right decisions are being made. This is driven by accountability measures and holding team members to account

- Set up working groups that are assigned time to work on process and technical improvements

- Make sure innovation focuses on removal or reduction of debt as part of organizational practices

- Celebrate when debt is removed without causing issues for the organization

- Track the costs saved through removing or reducing debt

- Ensure that with all new processes, innovations or technical solutions, there is a focus on removing debt as part of the process. Do not allow speed to market to deter you from removing debt in your estate

- Because debt eventually needs to be paid back, address it up front, to ensure there will be less debt later on.

Increased retention

The aim of increased staff retention is to ensure that any intellectual property that is gained during an employee's tenure with the organization is not lost. Retaining competent staff ensures greater efficiencies. If the following items are implemented, staff will feel empowered and will know that they have a voice in the growth and success of the organization:

- Set up communities of practice that all staff members are part of. These communities of practice are responsible for the efficiency of the ways of working, publishing any changes and training everyone in the practice

- Make sure staff sentiment is understood by reading exit feedback and taking this on board. Make changes across the organization, not just at one layer or within one team. Share feedback with all, to gain the maximum benefit from it

- Create a psychologically safe workplace,[51] with the foundation of empowerment and open communications at its core

- Hire for skill and diversity of thought. If biases are filtering in, follow up with training to help hiring teams understand the hiring practices needed.

Embedding the fourth principle: Alignment

The final principle is more than just organizational strategy. It relies on an agreed organizational structure, departmental planning and overarching strategies. It ensures full alignment across the organization regardless of where an individual or team may sit. Many leaders do not understand the need to have a team strategy, and often rely on the overarching business strategy. This is a failing that impacts the team, the tier the team operates in and the organization's ability to outperform its competitors.

The three elements that support the implementation of this principle are set out below.

Organizational strategy

Every successful organization has a strategy that grows and develops with it. Many strategies are revisited only on a three-to-five-year basis, but as industries are facing rapid change, the 10×Generation state suggests that strategy re-alignment should take place on a regular basis, with a cadence that works for the business but is more frequent than every three to five years.

The development of the strategy is performed across the organization, and its importance is explained to all, with the following options to draw on:

- Make sure growth targets in the organizational and departmental strategies exceed expectations
- Make the strategy inspirational but achievable, to set a clearly defined anchor point
- Ensure all stakeholders (that is, everyone in the organization) understand the importance of organizational alignment – how every decision will impact efficiency and delivery gains – with the overall strategy
- Bring together the operational team members to work 'side by side', to understand the pain points from the start of the product cycle. If each team has input into the outcomes, all voices will be heard
- Develop delivery goals that will be unique to your organization, and measure these outcomes as part of the overarching strategy. Here are suggestions to focus on, but note that the outcomes will depend on your market and type or business:
  - Value
  - Velocity
  - Quality
  - Reliability
- Because leadership focuses on breaking down barriers between teams, and this becomes a measure of success for the entire organization, bring back the empowerment experienced in the startup to the operational layer
- Consider security and risk, and create targets to address these areas in the strategy.

Departmental strategy

As with the organizational strategy, the departmental strategy is developed as a collaborative action. Being included in the decision-making process creates an enthusiasm across the team, and brings the vision into the forefront of team and individual thinking. Here are some ideas to help with the process:

- Documenting the strategy for the department is a collaborative process and ensures that all individuals are part of the process
- Collaboration instils buy-in across all layers
- As per the organizational strategy, all departments, teams and individuals are stakeholders and need to be taken through the strategy, to garner buy-in and ensure that direction is clear.

Defined organizational design

In contrast with having a flat or a tall organization structure, the 10×Generation state is one where there is overlap across departments and tiers. This overlap provides the required visibility for all, and removes bottlenecks and hierarchies. The options needed to bring the organization cohesion are as follows:

- Make sure product and technology are seen as one and are never separated. Separating these two key foundational areas would create hurdles that would hamper progress and growth
- Create visibility by having all teams understand where they fit into the design
- Be sure to understand the organizational structure to support the operational layer, or the 'engine room', as this is key to the organization's success. The engine room creates the foundation for all other departments to flow from.

The 10×Generation organizational design

Figure 21 shows the organizational framework known as the 10×Generation structure. In this structure, each departmental layer is interconnected, facilitating communication lines that span across all levels. While each department operates independently, it does so with a clear understanding of its respective roles, responsibilities and accountabilities, all the while maintaining a collective awareness of its position in the larger organization and how its contributions contribute to the overall mission.

This holistic perspective fosters cross-functional collaboration, reducing barriers to communication and enhancing visibility. Roles are grouped into distinct departments irrespective of seniority, promoting the formation of cross-functional teams where every individual can actively participate. This structural design promotes a seamless collaborative approach across operational, tactical and strategic aspects. Each functional area maintains its internal focus but does not fall into the trap of isolation, ultimately resulting in the organization sharing a unified vision that holds the potential for exponential growth.

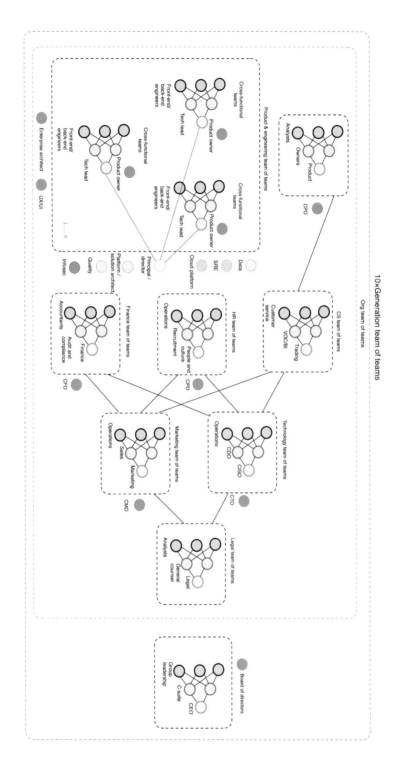

Figure 21 The 10×Generation organizational design

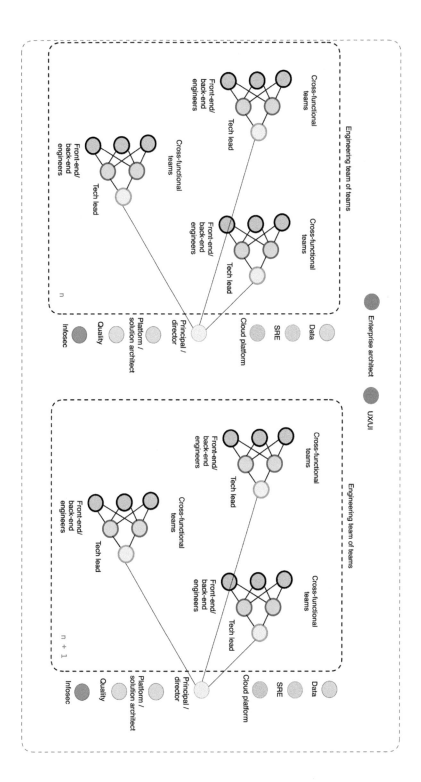

Figure 22 The operational engine room

The operational engine room structure

The engine room serves as the central operational hub housing the IT function. In this hub, critical support is provided to the organization, establishing a foundation for expansion. Given that IT is an essential requirement for all organizations, structuring it in a manner that promotes seamless communication among all IT teams is instrumental in facilitating the realization of the organization's growth strategy (Figure 22).

When this central hub is interconnected with the tactical layer, which comprises individual departments, a profound understanding of department-specific needs and the corresponding challenges to address comes into focus. It also becomes evident how the operational aspect can effectively cater for these requirements. Simultaneously, the strategic layer gains a clear understanding of the obstacles that impact both the operational and tactical layers, thereby discerning the necessary measures to support both aspects of the organization.

The tactical department structure

The tactical framework illustrates how departments will communicate with each other. These intersection points serve as catalysts for enhanced visibility and the exchange of innovative ideas among departments, fostering a bridge of comprehension with the engine room. Through promoting open lines of communication, articulating issues and innovation requirements, we begin to witness a reduction in 'shadow IT' practices, the emergence of improved solutions tailored to specific departmental requirements, and a heightened awareness of the support required between the operational and tactical layers (see Figure 23).

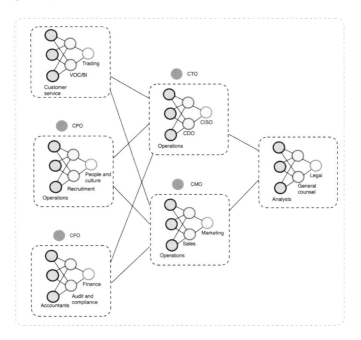

Figure 23 The tactical departments

The strategic executive structure

The ultimate tier is the strategic or executive perspective (Figure 24), which upholds an equivalent level of visibility and innovation exchange to those of the preceding layers. However, the primary objective at this level is to perpetuate strategic thinking and ensure that the organization is on track to achieve its established objectives. Similarly to the tactical and operational layers, this stratum will persist in maintaining open avenues of communication whenever feasible, persistently pursuing and reinforcing alignment throughout the organization.

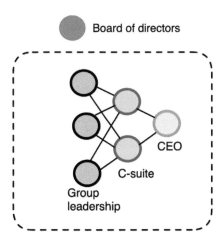

Figure 24 The executive

The 10×Generation state is one of autonomy, visibility and cross-functional collaboration. It is a place where the organization's vision is truly embedded and the structure provides open channels of communication for all. It celebrates innovation while ensuring problems are solved collaboratively, with an awareness of departmental needs and organizational growth aspirations.

9 Conclusion

From the time an organization breathes its first breath to the time that it transitions from startup to scaleup and so on, it will eventually suffer from the same three issues if they are not considered in the forefront of everyone's thinking throughout its growth:

- A misalignment of structure
- The use of digital transformations as an alternative to addressing poor performance
- Silos among departments reducing visibility.

Each scenario in Chapter 7 was taken from the authors' collective experience. The solutions proposed at the end of each script are documented to guide you in your journey to a better way of operating.

The intent is to provide you first with a different way of thinking, and then with a way of adopting the changes in a controlled manner to ensure that everyone is taken on the journey, together. If you do not address the issues up front, the people and process bloat will continue to permeate the organization as it grows. If you are in an SMB or enterprise, you may already be experiencing the impacts of people and process excess. If this is the case, knowing that there is a better way of operating may provide the options you seek but have never considered until now.

The old way of addressing issues has been to throw people at the problem. For many leaders, this will continue to be the first option, and for many it will be the only option considered. As leaders attempt to improve efficiencies, there will be the temptation to transform ways of working by embarking on a digital transformation. However, as we have explained in depth, understanding what a digital transformation is can be the challenge, as this can be different from organization to organization. A digital transformation will never achieve what the business had hoped for if the objectives are not clear to begin with. Many will stay on this merry-go-round until someone with the courage to offer another option steps into the fray.

Knowing your stage

Let's revisit the opening analogy for a moment. Do you know which stage you are at?

If you are at the *boarding* stage, your operational state or engine room should be a highly efficient function in your organization. All the ground crew are clear as to what needs to happen for a passenger to board the aircraft. The ways of working are understood in the operational tier, and the product and services roadmap is known from this perspective. The flight crew is preparing the plane for take-off and doing all of its pre-flight checks.

Your customers have embarked on this journey with you before and believe they know what to expect. If your engine room is running efficiently, this expectation can be easily met. But if it is not, you may need to focus on this aspect to ensure that your organization's foundational layer is shored up.

If you are at *take-off*, your operational state or engine room will be a highly efficient function in your organization, communicating strongly with the tactical tier. All ways of working are understood and there is very clear direction for what each individual is doing and what they are achieving, and an overall synergy across the operational and tactical tiers. The flight controllers know exactly which plane is ready to take off. The cabin crew has armed doors and cross-checked, and the flight is ready to go.

In your organization, your customers know your products, are happy with your services and are eagerly waiting to embark on the next journey with you, whether that be a new product launch or an increase in services. As you taxi down the runway, your passengers are strapped in and ready to go. However, if there are disparate processes that do not link the ground crew with the flight crew, you will have miscommunication, which can be disastrous. Connecting the operational and tactical tiers will ensure that the flight gets in the air safely as the organization makes its way to cruising altitude.

If you are at *cruising altitude*, all three tiers will be working effectively. There will be an understanding of how each department functions, and communication will be clear. All organizations strive to reach cruising altitude, as this is where you have a solid flight path, away from other flights, and are travelling at over 500 mph. Your destination rapidly approaches. To ensure that the destination is clear, everyone across the organization has visibility of the mission and vision set at the strategic tier, and is fully invested in them.

There is an intrinsic knowledge that everyone is working towards the common goals and working together. If you are still impacted by silos and endless bureaucracy, it may be hard to reach cruising altitude. Imagine that the flight controllers do not your destination and cannot clear a flight pathway. This is analogous to the operational layer not having a clear view of the product or services roadmap; if this is the case, how do they pave the way for innovation?

Being at cruising altitude means that you are producing more and creating greater value for your customers. If you are not there yet, there is work to be done. To take the next step, you need to know where you are in order to plot a pathway to success. This is the time when you should invest in a new approach.

When should I use this publication?

This guide was never intended to be read and then placed on a shelf to gather dust. It was written with the express hope that you would refer to the lessons in it at different moments during your organizational changes.

The authors believe that the best times to return to the publication are when:

- You can see that the organization is experiencing people or process bloat (or both)
- The leadership team in your organization decides to undertake a digital transformation to address its delivery and growth concerns
- You have been promoted from operational to tactical, from tactical to strategic, or from strategic to board
- You are starting a new role in the C-suite and want to be armed with the most up-to-date organizational thinking
- You are involved in an acquisition of another organization
- You simply want to know what senior executives are thinking about, and what they are relying on to fix problems.

You can revisit this guide at any point in your career journey, as it provides a view of different roles at different levels in an effort to provide a holistic viewpoint on an organization.

Going exponential!

The aim of this publication is to help organizations shift from old ways of structuring their business to a way that enables extraordinary growth – being able to break free from the atmosphere and push to the stars. This is possible if they embed a new way of operating – a new way of thinking – and bring the entire organization along the journey.

The solutions proposed at the end of each script in Chapter 7 are not exhaustive, but are designed to give you an idea of what can be implemented to solve similar problems, and will bring to life the 10×Generation state. The four principles become the starting point for an organization that wants to change and improve but isn't sure how. Each principle has defined actions that are taken and the order to proceed in. The very first step in any transformation, however, will be to convince the organization you work in that this is the best way to proceed.

Start thinking about how exciting it would be to alter your flight path, to fire rocket boosters, point your nose to the stars and burst through the atmosphere. This is the vision of the 10×Generation state; it is possible with the organization behind it, and will be the basis of your business case. Get the executive team or board excited by the possibility of where the change could take you.

Begin by understanding the scenarios and how they may be impacting your organization right now. Document your current state and how this is affecting your market share, your profitability, your customers and your employees. This will become the basis of the discussion you will need to have.

Just as you would build a business case for a programme of work, the same thing will be needed to gain buy-in for a metamorphosis of this kind. Once a proposed plan is in place and the benefits are defined, then and only then can you embark on what will be an organization-wide change.

The need for a revolution is upon us, and this publication provides the individual with the tools to make it possible. The time is now to rethink how our organizations work, how they improve and how they empower their greatest asset – their people.

The organization's leaders need to stop thinking of people as a cost on a profit-and-loss report, and instead think of the innovation they represent. Think of harnessing their potential and rewarding them for it. Make the workplace equitable for all, not just those at the executive level. Allow everyone to be a decision maker, a solution provider and an architect of their career.

The vision of the 10×Generation state is to provide everyone with the tools to curate their career, impact the strategic direction of the organization they work in and be empowered to innovate. This is an all-or-nothing approach – as is any revolution – and needs to be considered carefully.

If you are contented with the way your organization operates, this is not for you. But if you want more market share with greater innovation, and you want to be 'that organization' (you know the one: the one that keeps pipping the competition at the post), and quarter-on-quarter results that are the envy of everyone in your sector: if you want all of that, the time for change is upon you.

As Eckhart Tolle states: 'Awareness is the greatest agent for change.'[52] The greatest gift you can give your people, working in these environments, is a heightened level of awareness, to enable growth.

Helping others

We believe that this publication could help many individuals and companies struggling with throughput – those consumed by endless bureaucracy and sinking under the weight of excessive bloat.

We wrote this publication to help others, as we know that there is another way, a better way.

If you want others to experience the 10×Generation state, tell them about this guide.

Tell your friends, tell your work family – don't keep this to yourself.

It takes one person to start a movement. Be that person!

Ady Kalra and Mary-Beth Hosking

Endnotes

1 Medium. Eckhart Tolle's most important saying: 'Awareness is the greatest agent for change.' **https://medium.com/change-your-mind/eckhart-tolles-most-important-saying-awareness-is-the-greatest-agent-for-change-21e713d64a90** [accessed 12 October 2023]

2 iSixSigma website. **https://www.isixsigma.com/** [accessed 04 October 2023]

3 Gartner. Digitalisation strategy for business transformation. **https://www.gartner.com.au/en/information-technology/insights/digitalization** [accessed 04 October 2023]

4 MIT. The MIT Initiative on the Digital Economy (IDE): Shaping a brighter digital future. **https://ide.mit.edu** [accessed 04 October 2023]

5 Intelligence Resource Program. Joint Publication 1: Doctrine for the armed forces of the United States. **https://irp.fas.org/doddir/dod/jp1.pdf**; Joint Publication 3-0: Joint operations. **https://irp.fas.org/doddir/dod/jp3_0.pdf** [both accessed 04 October 2023]

6 Flexera. State of the cloud report (2022). **https://path.flexera.com/cm/report-state-of-the-** [accessed 04 October 2023]

7 Merholz, P. and Skinner, K. (2016). *Org Design for Design Orgs: Building and managing in-house design teams*. O'Reilly Media, Sebastopol, California.

8 Agile Manifesto. Principles behind the Agile Manifesto. **https://agilemanifesto.org/principles.html** [accessed 05 October 2023]

9 Atlassian. DevOps. **https://www.atlassian.com/devops** [accessed 05 October 2023]

10 IBM. What is DevSecOps? **https://www.ibm.com/topics/devsecops** [accessed 05 October 2023]

11 BMC. Agile vs waterfall SDLCs: What's the difference? **https://www.bmc.com/blogs/agile-vs-waterfall/** [accessed 05 October 2023]

12 iSixSigma website. **https://www.isixsigma.com/** [accessed 04 October 2023]

13 *New York Post*. Twitter co-founder Jack Dorsey apologizes: 'I realize many are angry with me'. **https://nypost.com/2022/11/05/twitter-co-founder-jack-dorsey-apologizes/** [accessed 05 October 2023]

14 GoLeanSixSigma.com. 8 Wastes. **https://goleansixsigma.com/8-wastes/** [accessed 05 October 2023]

15 MIT Center for Information Systems Research. Empowering employees to build value in a digital world: Case study – DBS digital capabilities. **https://cisr.mit.edu/publication/dbs-digital-capabilities** [accessed 05 October 2023]

16 Nadkarni, S. and Prugl, R. (2020). Digital transformation: a review, synthesis and opportunities for future research. *Management Review Quarterly*, vol.71(2), 233–341.

17 Drucker Institute. Measurement myopia. **https://www.drucker.institute/thedx/measurement-myopia/** [accessed 05 October 2023]

18 Premier Agile. The three pillars of empiricism. **https://premieragile.com/the-three-pillars-of-empiricism/** [accessed 05 October 2023]

19 *MIT Sloan Management Review*. Creativity in decision making with value-focused thinking. **https://sloanreview.mit.edu/article/creativity-in-decision-making-with-valuefocused-thinking/** [accessed 05 October 2023]

20 Forbes. 'If you can't measure it, you can't manage it': not true. **https://www.forbes.com/sites/lizryan/2014/02/10/if-you-cant-measure-it-you-cant-manage-it-is-bs/?sh=27bdd6cf7b8b** [accessed 05 October 2023]

21 wiseGEEK. What is organizational design theory? **https://www.wise-geek.com/what-is-organizational-design-theory.htm** [accessed 05 October 2023]

22 Embroker Insurance Services. 106 must-know startup statistics for 2023. **https://www.embroker.com/blog/startup-statistics/** [accessed 05 October 2023]

23 Flow Research Collective website. **https://www.flowresearchcollective.com** [accessed 05 October 2023]

24 Staind. *Not Again* (lyrics on Genius). **https://genius.com/Staind-not-again-lyrics** [accessed 05 October 2023]

25 Gartner. Gartner says the majority of technology products and services will be built by professionals outside of IT by 2024. **https://www.gartner.com/en/newsroom/press-releases/2021-06-10-gartner-says-the-majority-of-technology-products-and-services-will-be-built-by-professionals-outside-of-it-by-2024** [accessed 05 October 2023]

26 Seeking Mastery. Make 'disagree and commit' work for you. **https://seekingmastery.wordpress.com/2017/05/29/make-disagree-and-commit-work-for-you/** [accessed 06 October 2023]

27 Investopedia. The Peter Principle: What it is and how to overcome it. **https://www.investopedia.com/terms/p/peter-principle.asp** [accessed 06 October 2023]

28 Franklin Covey. Big rocks – Stephen R. Covey. **https://resources.franklincovey.com/the-8th-habit/big-rocks-stephen-r-covey** [accessed 06 October 2023]

29 Jobs, S. (2011). *His own Words and Wisdom*. Cupertino Silicon Valley Press.

30 Gartner. Driving action with NPS and other loyalty metrics: Focusing on key success factors. **https://www.gartner.com/en/documents/3782181** [accessed 06 October 2023]

31 Collins English Dictionary. Definition of 'Dobbing'. **https://www.collinsdictionary.com/us/dictionary/english/dobbing** [accessed 09 October 2023]

32 Time-Management-Abilities.com. The POSEC Method of time management. **https://www.time-management-abilities.com/posec-method.html** [accessed 09 October 2023]

33 The Product Manager. What is value vs effort matrix and how does it work in product management? **https://theproductmanager.com/topics/value-vs-effort-matrix/** [accessed 07 November 2023]

34 Ladder. ICE Framework: Scoring tactics would get you killed on the battlefield. **https://ladder.io/blog/growth-strategy** [accessed 09 October 2023]

35 Jim Collins. First who, then what. **https://www.jimcollins.com/concepts/first-who-then-what.html** [accessed 09 October 2023]

36 Grammarly. Sunk cost fallacy: Definition and examples. **https://www.grammarly.com/blog/sunk-cost-fallacy/** [accessed 09 October 2023]

37   Simplicable. Mushroom Management. **https://management.simplicable.com/management/new/mushroom-management** [accessed 10 October 2023]

38   AZquotes. Middle management quotes. **https://www.azquotes.com/quotes/topics/middle-management.html** [accessed 10 October 2023]

39   Gartner. Changing behaviors: From working in silos to working collaboratively. **https://www.gartner.com/en/doc/3887366-changing-behaviors-from-working-in-silos-to-working-collaboratively** [accessed 10 October 2023]

40   George, M. L., Rowlands, D., and Kastle, B. (2004). *What is Lean Six Sigma?* McGraw-Hill, New York.

41   International Organization for Standardization (ISO). Quality management principles. **https://www.iso.org/files/live/sites/isoorg/files/store/en/PUB100080.pdf** [accessed 10 October 2023]

42   IBM. What is IT Infrastructure Library (ITIL)? **https://www.ibm.com/topics/it-infrastructure-library** [accessed 10 October 2023]

43   ISACA (2018). *COBIT 2019 Framework: Introduction and methodology.*

44   The Open Group. Welcome to TOGAF™ – The Open Group Architecture Framework. **https://pubs.opengroup.org/architecture/togaf8-doc/arch/** [accessed 10 October 2023]

45   McChrystal, S. (2015). *Team of Teams: New rules of engagement for a complex world.* Penguin General, UK.

46   Gartner. Manage technology debt to create technology wealth. **https://www.gartner.com/en/documents/3989188** [accessed 10 October 2023]

47   Forrester. Forget about build versus buy; your choice is customize or compose. **https://www.forrester.com/report/forget-about-build-versus-buy-your-choice-is-customize-or-compose/RES162576** [accessed 10 October 2023]

48   Deloitte. Technology and the boardroom: A CIO's guide to engaging the board. **https://www2.deloitte.com/us/en/insights/focus/cio-insider-business-insights/boards-technology-fluency-cio-guide.html** [accessed 11 October 2023]

49   Onboard. What are board member roles and responsibilities? **https://www.onboardmeetings.com/blog/board-member-roles-responsibilities/** [accessed 11 October 2023]

50   Statista (2023). Mergers and acquisitions (M&As) worldwide – statistics and facts. **https://www.statista.com/topics/1146/mergers-and-acquisitions/#topicOverview** [accessed 7 November 2023]

51   Center for Creative Leadership. What is psychological safety at work? How leaders can build psychologically safe workplaces. **https://www.ccl.org/articles/leading-effectively-articles/what-is-psychological-safety-at-work/** [accessed 12 October 2023]

52   Medium. Eckhart Tolle's most important saying: 'Awareness is the greatest agent for change.' **https://medium.com/change-your-mind/eckhart-tolles-most-important-saying-awareness-is-the-greatest-agent-for-change-21e713d64a90** [accessed 12 October 2023]

Index